Joy... Anyway!

CAROLYN LUNN

Beacon Hill Press of Kansas City
Kansas City, Missouri

To
Vernon
Sharon and Bill, Aubrey and Ashley
Susan and Paul, Carter and Crystal
Kevin and Kathy

Photo: Steve Attig

Row 1 (left to right)
Sharon, Aubrey and Ashley Clair; Carolyn Lunn;
Crystal, Carter, and Susan Clem
Row 2
Bill Clair; Kevin and Kathleen Lunn; Vernon Lunn; Paul
Clem

*"You and I were created for joy,
and if we miss it, we miss
the reason for our existence. . . .
If our joy is honest joy,
it must somehow be
congruous with human tragedy.
This is the test of joy's integrity:
Is it compatible with pain?
Only the heart that hurts
has a right to joy."*[1]

LEWIS SMEDES

Contents

Acknowledgments

Goethe said: "To put your ideas into action is the most difficult thing in the world."

It's a risky thing to put your innermost thoughts on paper. It makes you unbelievably vulnerable. But God in His beautiful timing made me ready. My brother-in-law, Chuck Millhuff, in his inimitable way, called me one day and said, "Carolyn, I've been thinking and praying a lot about it, and I feel it's time for you to write your book. Let's set up a breakfast date with Harold Ivan Smith and talk to him about it. He's a good writer and well-published author, and he'll be able to tell us the steps necessary to prepare a book for publishing. Write an introduction and outline that we can present to him."

After reading my outline, Harold encouraged me to write. He shared with us the steps he felt I should take and recommended Bonnie Perry to work with me as an editor. What a happy relationship this has been! I thank Bonnie, for without her dedication to the project, her professional insights, and belief in me when the going was difficult, this book could not have been written. And thank you, Chuck and Harold.

My family has been incredible. Vernon has done all the cooking and laundry while I wrote. He has believed in me and encouraged me every step of the way. He is one of the most unselfish people I have ever known. Each of my children in their own unique way have given love and support. I love you, dear family!

Thank you needs to be expressed also to all those at Beacon Hill Press of Kansas City who believed in the book and worked so hard to bring it to press, including Paul Skiles, Hardy Weathers, and the members of the Book Committee.

Introduction

This book could not have been written until now. It has taken time to gain perspective, to see the intriguing pattern of the mercy and loving-kindness of my sovereign Lord. To wonder anew at the way He repeatedly prepared me ahead of time for the "bigger than life" crisis moments. It is a story of the sometimes unfathomable realities of life. It is my personal theology becoming real as I scuffed along on the sandy, sometimes rocky, road of life. It is the principles I believe, working themselves out in practice.

Sometimes I have stumbled and fallen and rubbed my nose in the sand before I was able to reach up and take my Savior's hand. But there have been times also when I could walk tall with serenity and peace through the darkest moments because I had learned He is always there—in the shadows as well as the light—and He can be trusted, because He loves me with a love greater than I can comprehend!

God has laughed with me, cried with me, reasoned with me, chastised me, encouraged me, empowered me! He has used a fascinating array of interesting people to impact my life. You will meet some of them in the pages ahead.

I am a voracious reader. Therefore, I am sure that the concepts and ideas I have read have been integrated into my value system. Where possible, I try to faithfully give credit; but if I fail, please understand that I cannot remember when or where the thought was learned.

There is one central thought I would like to convey as I write. I have learned that you need not be afraid to walk, not run, right up to reality and *face it head-on;* for no matter what that reality may be, our God, who is the "Wonderful Counselor, Mighty God, Everlasting Father, Prince of Peace" (Isa. 9:6), *will be there!* His arms will enfold us, His wisdom will teach us, His power will enable us, and His love and mercy will enrich us; we will *never* be alone. We need not fear one who loves us so perfectly!

And there is *joy, anyway!* Indescribable, all-encompassing joy. I am learning to look for it, to count on it, to know its healing power.

In the pages ahead I hope I will be able to share His way so that you won't miss the joy on *your* journey with God!

*"My assumption is that
the story of any one of us
is in some measure
the story of us all."*[2]

FREDERICK BUECHNER

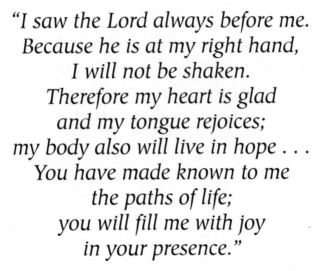

"I saw the Lord always before me.
Because he is at my right hand,
I will not be shaken.
Therefore my heart is glad
and my tongue rejoices;
my body also will live in hope . . .
You have made known to me
the paths of life;
you will fill me with joy
in your presence."

ACTS 2:25-26, 28

■ıı 1

A God Who Draws Near

Every affliction comes with a message
from the heart of God.   ALEXANDER MACLAREN

As I maneuvered my car into the parking place in front of the medical center, I inwardly acknowledged that I was coming to this appointment reluctantly. If it had not been for the tingling and aching in my right arm that extended down into my hand, I knew I would not be here now. But once before, I had experienced a similar sensation, and doctors had discovered a lump under my arm that subsequently had to be removed. Thankfully, it had been benign, but this familiar pain was not something I could ignore.

It was a sunny, cool February day, but my heart sank with trepidation as I pushed through the revolving door. The heels of my shoes clicked sharply as I crossed the tiled foyer. I recalled that as a child I used to listen to ladies walking in their high heels and hear the clicking sound and long for the day when I, too, could wear heels. It meant somehow that you had arrived at the wonderful state of womanhood. Little did I realize all that maturity could bring, I thought.

The information desk clerk directed me to the Imaging Department for my mammogram. They were expecting me. As I walked into the Imaging section, a young, dark-haired technician came forward and introduced herself to me as Susan.

"That will be an easy name for me to remember," I told her, "because I have a daughter named Susan."

Smiling, she led me back to a small dressing area and gave me a light blue smock. I watched somewhat apprehensively as Susan prepared the machine. When she was ready, she explained in careful detail exactly what she needed to do and gently worked with me to attain the results. Susan was professional, yet considerate. When she finished, she gathered the heavy glass and metal plates from the machine and turned to leave the room.

In a short time, she returned and said, "I will need to get a couple more pictures. The doctor wants to be sure he has all he needs." After she finished, she said, "It shouldn't be very long." And she left me alone in the room again.

But this time the wait was longer. As Susan walked back into the room, she hesitated a moment and then slowly walked toward me. She diffidently stroked the lapel of her lab coat, and somehow I knew something was wrong.

"Mrs. Lunn," she said, "the doctor would like to have your permission to look at the plates from your last mammogram. They were not taken at this hospital, were they?"

"No, they were taken in Michigan," I said. "We moved here to Kansas City in September."

"Would you call Michigan and ask the hospital to send the plates to us as soon as possible?"

"Is there a lump, Susan?" I asked her.

"I really can't say," she said, "but the doctor would

like to see the plates to determine if there has been a change since last year or if the image he sees is common for you. After he reads the plates, we will let you know."

"I am a speaker," I told her, "and I am to speak for three days in Ohio, and then I am scheduled to go to Florida for four days of rest with my husband. Since I will not be able to know the results of the test for a few days, it would probably be well for me to go ahead with my plans, don't you think?"

"Yes," she said. "I'll make a note to call you in seven days. Your own physician will receive the results also."

When I left the hospital, I was so disturbed I couldn't even remember where my car was parked. I stopped at the edge of the small parking lot. Had I driven my car or my husband's? I glanced around the lot, trying to spot one of them, and saw my car parked in the second row.

I looked down as I stepped off the curb and slowly walked to my car. I watched my feet plod one after the other, each seeming too heavy to lift for the next step. I reached the car and tried to concentrate enough to remember the combination to the car lock. Finally, the lock clicked open, and I stepped inside. Automatically putting on my seat belt and inserting my key in the ignition, I started for home.

Driving more slowly than I usually do, I headed north on the interstate. But just before I reached my exit, I looked at the clock on the dashboard and realized I could not go home. I had another doctor's appointment scheduled in only 30 minutes. I had nearly forgotten.

My next appointment was at the Osteoporosis Center. Recently my endocrinologist had suggested I have an exam to check for osteoporosis. As I drove, it seemed as though my heart and mind had slipped into neutral—that was the only way I could keep moving. I did not deal with what I had learned. If I could only accomplish the next task, then I could think, evaluate, and cope.

At the doctor's office in the clinic, the nurse technician was warm and friendly. She led me into a room where the only furniture was a long, narrow table over which a large X-ray instrument was poised, a metal chair, and a desk topped with a computer and a printer. The technician helped me onto the table and explained the procedure. For nearly 30 minutes I was to lie still on the table as the machine went from one end of my body to the other, scanning the density of my bones. After preparing the machine and checking the computer, she started the test and quietly left the room.

I watched the machine for a while, but it moved slowly and there was absolutely no sensation, so I lost interest. Soon I drifted off to a light sleep, but when the technician came back into the room I awoke instantly. Sitting in the lone chair, she took a long sheet of paper and began to ask me questions about my diet and exercise habits. When she was finished, the machine had completed its work also, and she helped me get off the table.

The technician sat at the computer and began to translate the findings of the test onto a graph sheet. I stood and watched but could not understand the medical technology. I *could* tell from her facial expressions and an occasional low murmur that the findings might be different than I had hoped. After she finished working with the computer, she turned to me and, pointing to the screen, began to show me the specific place in my hip where osteoporosis had weakened the bone. She explained that the doctor would look at the findings to determine how severely the disease had affected me. He would give the results to my endocrinologist, who would prescribe the treatment.

I was especially distressed by the changed attitude of the technician. When I entered the office, she was lighthearted and cheerful. Now, she was still warm, but very solicitous, as though she were afraid I might fall and break. She took my weight and height. When she said 5 feet 6 inches, I said, "Oh, no, you must have that wrong, I've always been a little more than 5 feet 7 inches."

So she measured again but said, "No, that was right. You are only 5 feet 6 inches."

I was shocked. Already, I had lost more than one inch in height!

The nurse handed me a book given to all patients with osteoporosis, and I left the office. As I started down the hall, I glanced through it. Pictures of women with stooped shoulders. Graphs with explanations about the fragility of bones. Warnings about the hazards of falling. Suddenly the words and pictures began to blur, and my throat felt raw as I struggled to keep from dissolving in a flood of tears. Stopping at a pay phone in the hall, I called my husband, Vernon. My words were barely audible as they fought their way through my tears. I told him what had happened at both of the appointments. I was so distraught that I could barely articulate my feelings. He was tender and told me to come home—we would face it all together.

As I drove home in the late afternoon sun, I wept. I thought of all the wonderful plans Vernon and I had made. We had been looking forward to this next passage of our lives. Vernon is older than I and had recently retired from the company that employed him for 24 years. He had been with Alexander Hamilton Life Insurance Company from its early beginnings and had been a part of its growth to a giant in its industry. He had been a member of the Board of Directors, and at retirement he was senior vice president of corporate services and human resources. His business career had been interesting and challenging, and we had made wonderful friends along the way. We had been in Michigan for 22 years, but after Vernon's retirement we decided to move to Kansas City. All three of our children lived there, and we wanted to be near them.

So we had built a beautiful new home. It was the home I had always dreamed of having. It wasn't as big as our home in Michigan, but it was perfect for our life now. I chose all new colors—different from those we had lived with so long. We purchased some new furniture. For the first time in my life, the day we moved in, the wallpapering and painting were completely done, and most of the window treatments were finished.

We were looking forward to a new adventure. I had been afraid that when Vernon retired, maybe he wouldn't want me to travel and speak; but he insisted that I not retire. I could continue to work in ministry. We loved being near our children and grandchildren. We loved our new church. We missed our close friends in Michigan, but we were renewing old friendships and making new ones. We were looking forward to doing some traveling.

And now this! As I continued to drive home, I visualized what I might look like in the future. The image I saw of myself was a short, bent-over, stoop-shouldered, frail woman with no breasts—and I was devastated!

As I pulled into the driveway of our home, my eyes were still clouded with tears. I drove into the garage, quickly got out of the car, and rushed into the house. Vernon met me in the kitchen and drew me into his arms. We didn't say anything. Finally, we went to sit in the living room and talk about all that had happened.

I knew my news was hard on Vernon. He had been through this before. His first wife had died with cancer. It was discovered first in her breast and then had gone into her pancreas. My heart ached for him. When we finished talking, Vernon wrapped his arms around me once again and began to pray. He prayed simply, in words that starkly expressed our feeling about the situation. He asked God for wisdom and peace and comfort, for His guidance every step of the way. He gave God the whole burden. He asked for hope—hope that perhaps there would be no cancer, but healing if there were.

Then I prayed. I asked God to help me focus on the

message and on Him as I went to Ohio to speak. I needed Him to enable and anoint me and to give me an inner serenity in this waiting period, to help me not to be so absorbed in my own anxiety that I could not minister to others. I prayed that somehow my inner concern would be turned into sensitivity to another's need, and God could use me as a healing agent for Him. When I finished praying, we just sat there quietly. I felt totally drained emotionally.

I went to Ohio. And as I spoke that week, the words took on special meaning to me. It seemed as though God illuminated the thoughts He had given me when everything was going well, and He made them live with vibrancy now in my hurting. I thought, You are speaking on the principles of living for Christ, and that which is happening in your life right now is the practice. It's the place where your belief takes hold and changes from just theology to life experience.

I didn't tell anyone on my trip the experience I was going through. It was too new. I was still working through it in my mind, as I had learned to do in other crises of my life in years gone by. I had learned to spend time alone with God, to stay in His presence, to allow Him to think through my thoughts and teach me what I needed to know. But right now, it seemed as though I was in a holding pattern. I felt I was just to wait, to allow Him to comfort my anxiety. This was not the first time reality's harsh wind had blown open the unsuspecting door of my heart. On many occasions its force had left me battered and torn. But oh, the power of knowing that the God of reality was already there, waiting to meet my need!

When I returned home, there was a message on our tape machine to call the medical center. Susan, the same technician who had taken the mammogram, told me in a few words:

"Mrs. Lunn, the doctor would like you to call Dr.

Rhoads, your surgeon. There is a lump in your right breast. He has forwarded the report to her, and she will advise you now. I'm sure I will see you again soon. I'll be thinking about you."

I thanked her for her kindness and hung up the phone.

Immediately I dialed the number of Dr. Rhoads's office and made an appointment to see her. The nurse was waiting for my call and gave me an appointment the next day. I went in search of Vernon to tell him.

At her office the next day, Dr. Rhoads sat down in a chair next to mine. Taking a piece of paper, she carefully drew a picture of my breast and explained to me where the lump was located.

"You will need to have an X ray taken of your breast once again, so that we can accurately locate the lump for the biopsy. It is so small that it could not be detected in any other way than through the mammogram. We will need to measure carefully to pinpoint the exact spot. Then you will need to go to outpatient surgery for the biopsy. We will schedule you right away.

"Only one out of nine women has breast cancer, Carolyn. You have no history of breast cancer in your family. The chances of your lump being benign are very good. And, the fact that it has been detected at an early stage is very important, no matter what the outcome."

"Did the pain in my right arm have any significance?" I asked.

"No, your arm aching had nothing to do with the diagnosis," she said.

"Well," I told her. "I believe God knows that that was the only thing that would alert me to the need to get the mammogram. I was overdue about six months, but when I felt that pain, I made an appointment immediately. It was His protective hand upon me again."

* * *

There was nothing glamorous about the mauve hospital gown I put on. I carefully folded it around me as I sat on the bed in the tiny, curtain-draped cubicle where we waited. The nurses and anesthesiologists had all come in to ask their many questions, and we were simply waiting for the time to come for me to be wheeled into surgery. A nurse in green surgical garb pushed open the door to the waiting area and headed for my cubicle. The moment had come! In silent dread, I turned to lie down on the bed. Vernon leaned over to kiss me, and I clung to his hand for just a moment. As the nurses wheeled me away, apprehension washed over me. When we entered the surgery, Dr. Rhoads was there, dressed in green surgical garb with her hands in surgical gloves held up, ready to work. The nurses helped me roll onto the surgery table, and I looked around the room for a moment at all the stainless steel equipment and the large lights over the operating table. I noticed it was cool enough in there to hang meat! The anesthesiologist stepped up to the table, and before I knew it, I was fading out of the picture.

When I woke up later in the recovery room, I was doing what I usually do after surgery. I was so nauseated, I was nearly overwhelmed with it! Just then, Dr. Rhoads walked into my cubical area with Vernon beside her. I took one look at his very white face, and I knew.

"Carolyn," Dr. Rhoads said, "your biopsy shows that the lump is malignant. Do you understand me?"

"Yes, I understand," I said. I was too sick to react very much.

Two days later, my daughter Sharon, who is a nurse, and I sat in the small waiting room in Dr. Rhoads's office. When Dr. Rhoads came in, she sat down and began to explain.

She presented three possible options for me to consider for treatment of my type of breast cancer, and then she recommended the procedure she felt would be best for me. Because my cancer had begun to spread into the milk ducts, she and the oncologist felt it would be best for me to have a modified radical mastectomy. They wanted me to give them permission to do a biopsy on the left breast also, during the surgery, because the kind of cancer I had, a great percentage of the time, mirrors itself in the other breast. If cell change or cancer were found, they wanted me to sign a consent to remove the other breast also. She told me to talk it over with my family, for my whole family would be affected by my decision.

That evening Vernon and I and our children gathered together and talked. We decided to follow Dr. Rhoads's advice. One phone call to her office, and the surgery was scheduled for two days later at 8 A.M.

I needed the next two days. There was a gnawing hunger inside of me to be alone with the Lord. I knew that only the wise counsel and loving-kindness of the Lord could bring me the inner peace I so deeply craved. You see, life's crises had taught me that when circumstances seem to rip apart my world, my own resources are not enough. Only God in His tender mercy has an unlimited supply of power available to meet me at the point of my need. I only need to come to Him and ask, to talk over these uncertain and confusing circumstances with Him.

There have been many life-changing crises in my life. Sometimes I have wondered why the Lord has allowed so many crises to come my way. Was I an especially selfish, insensitive person, so that that was the only way God could reach through to my heart? I don't know. Could it be that His main purpose was to use those life-changing pivot points to help me see Him as He really is? Through the crises I have discovered that He knew the places where I was bruised and in need of healing. Places that would make it impossible for me to see Him unless He intervened. Had His intervention helped me leap over the obstacles that would have blinded me so that I might know Him? Had His loving wisdom put an eternal perspective within my grasp?

God does that for each one of us. It is not necessary for everyone to experience what I have experienced in order to know God in all His fullness. You have not been bruised in the same areas as I. We each have our own needs, and He will help us know Him, with mercy and loving-kindness, in the way that is best for us.

Because of His guidance in years gone by, I knew that when my heart has been lacerated with pain and uncertainty, I had a need to be quiet and allow Him to speak to me. With a slow, weary tread I climbed the stairs to my loft study.

I sat in silence, thinking about God. He brought to my mind the story in the Old Testament of Joshua, the great leader who had followed Moses in leading the nation of Israel to the Promised Land. Just before He was ready to do a great miracle in parting the waters of the Jordan River for the Israelites, God had a long conversation with Joshua. He told him of the things they must do to prepare themselves for what He planned to do for them. One of the things God told Joshua was to appoint one man from each tribe for a special task. As they crossed the Jordan on the dry riverbed, each of the 12 men was to pick up a rock and carry it to the other side. The rocks, representing the 12 tribes, were to be used to build an altar. This altar was to forever remind them of the miracle God had wrought at this time.

As I meditated, it seemed as though God was encouraging me to review my life with Him, to pick up the precious stones that represented His sovereign hand in my life, to remember where He had intervened time and time again with His power and love. I had made a habit from the time I was in my teens to notate in my Bible the promises God had given me in His Word. By the verse of promise I would put the date and sometimes a word or two concerning the circumstances of need. By glancing through my Bibles, I had a spiritual autobiography at my fingertips, for the Bibles had been read consecutively, each one representing a slice of my life. There was a small red leather Bible, a green hardbacked Bible, a black leather Bible, and a dark red hardcover Bible.

I gathered all the Bibles together and sat down to read, beginning with the little red leather Bible. I leafed through the pages, looking for the notations—my precious stones of remembrance. As I began to read, the tears began to flow. I was filled with wonder and awe at the way, time and time again, He had prepared me for crises ahead without my even realizing it. His watchful care, His mighty power, His wise counsel were recorded in those under-lined verses.

For those two days, as I read and meditated and prayed, thanksgiving and joy pulsed through me. Here was the evidence! Again, I could walk right up to reality and not be afraid, for God had always been there to meet me at my point of need! He was not threatened by my questioning. He had always been there waiting, ready to enfold me in His love and power.

In her book *The Christian's Secret of a Happy Life,* Hannah Whitall Smith said,

> What we need . . . is to see that God's presence is a certain fact always, and that every act of our soul is done before Him, and that a word spoken in prayer is as really spoken to Him as if our eyes could see Him and our hands could touch Him. Then we shall cease to have such vague conceptions of our relations with Him, and shall feel the binding force of every word we say in His presence.[1]

My Bibles and devotional books I had used during

those times were a witness to that truth. I thought of the sense of inner joy brought to me in those times. I looked up the word *joy* in the dictionary, and it said,

"**Joy**/'joi **1**. *n*: the emotion evoked by well-being, success, or good fortune. **2**. *v*: to experience great pleasure or delight."[2]

But these definitions did not express my experience of joy. After some thinking, I wrote down my own definition:

Joy/: an indwelling, glad energy that inspires an inner serenity not dependent on outward circumstances; the fruit of intimate, vibrant relationship with God instead of aloneness.

This is what Jesus modeled before us. Jesus was a joyous man. Heb. 1:9 says He was "anointed . . . with the oil of gladness" (KJV).

No matter what His circumstances, He had learned joy, and John 15:11 says that Jesus came to earth "that your joy might be full" (KJV).

That is His promise to us. We can be anointed with joy even in the unfathomable realities of life.

That inner, serene joy carried me through four operations in the next year and a half in which both breasts were removed and breast restoration was done!

In the next chapter I will share the initial crisis that changed the direction of my life and began my preparation for life's journey. Then there's the . . . rest of the story of my incredible walk into joy.

*"Those who sow in tears
will reap with
songs of joy."*

PS. 126:5

A Shattering Moment

My life is a performance for which I was never given any chance to rehearse.[1]   ASHLEIGH BRILLIANT

All I could focus on was the pain—the unrelenting, excruciating, throbbing pain in my head. As I gradually came more and more to consciousness, I realized that though the most intense pain was in my head, my whole body was hurting. I'd never felt such pain. My first impulse was to try and move my arms and legs. I did move them, but it hurt.

My eyelids seemed too heavy to lift, so I tried to figure out where I was by the sounds around me. I heard the reedy, shrill voice of someone near me saying, "I want to be moved out of this room. I want to go now! She talks all the time! I can't sleep!"

Slowly I turned my head toward the sound and lifted weighted eyelids to see what was happening. I saw a nurse in a white uniform struggling with a tiny, frail, white-haired woman who was flailing about in her bed. The nurse was trying to soothe the older woman by promising to move her. As I thought about what the woman had said, I realized that I must be the person she was talking about. There were only two beds in the room. I wonder

31

what I said when I was doing all that talking, I thought. I hope I didn't say anything embarrassing!

Closing my eyes again, I listened to the other sounds around me. The disembodied voice on the paging system calling the names of doctors, the clanking sounds of carts moving down the hall, and the muffled sound of conversation. I realized I was in a hospital. Struggling to think, I tried to concentrate enough to put the pieces together, but I couldn't. Slowly I slipped into unconsciousness.

Sometime during that period of unconsciousness I gathered from conversation around me that they believed I was gravely injured. Anxiety came over me. Would I die? I knew I was a Christian, but I was afraid of the unknown way to heaven. What was the process of death? Would Jesus be right there as I passed from this world to the other? I felt the gathering shackles of fear.

In that moment, in that hospital room when I was all alone and afraid, God came. He brought to my memory a Scripture verse I had learned as a little child. "Yea, though I walk through the valley of the shadow of death, I will fear no evil: for thou art with me; thy rod and thy staff they comfort me" (Ps. 23:4, KJV). As those words sank into my soul, peace came to me, and I could literally feel the pressure of God's arms around me giving me comfort. In that moment He took all my fear away! Amazingly, I was at peace! I drifted into a quiet rest.

Sometime later, I briefly awoke. At the end of my bed stood a figure clad in white, and I remember thinking, I made it! But it wasn't an angel—it was the mother superior of the Catholic hospital in which I found myself!

* * *

It was late afternoon. The sun was low in the sky, and the shadow from the branches of the tree outside my window was silhouetted against the wall. I had regained consciousness once again and looked around the room. I was alone now. My heart was heavy, but I didn't know why. My mind was not able to think logically, to piece together why I was there. It was so hard to stay awake. I heard someone walking into the room, and I opened my eyes to see a white-coated doctor with a metal clipboard in his hand and another shorter man.

My head hurt so badly, I could hardly focus my eyes on them. I felt a deep sense of foreboding as I waited to see what the doctor had to say.

"Carolyn," he said, "this is Pastor Reed. He is a pastor from a local church. He has come to see you.

"You are no doubt wondering what has happened," he continued. "At 4:30 this morning, you were in an automobile accident. You were brought to this hospital. You are in Hannibal, Mo. You have been unconscious most of the day, but whenever you would briefly come to consciousness, you would ask about your husband, and we know you are distressed about him. Carolyn, he was killed in that accident."

Awful black emptiness washed over me. Pain seemed to rip my heart apart. As darkness slowly began to envelop me, I heard the pastor begin to pray. I never heard the prayer's conclusion.

Later, I heard firm steps approaching the door of my room. My bed was near the window on the far side of the room, and I watched as my father and mother entered and walked quickly to my bedside.

"Daddy," I said. "David's dead."

"I know, Honey," he said.

Then my father bent over the bed and drew me into his arms as I cried heartbrokenly. Mother stood there as I clung to my father, looking at me lovingly. I felt comforted. We talked for a while, but I soon grew tired. Dad left the room to call David's parents about the funeral arrangements. Mother stayed in the room with me. She sat knitting in a chair in the corner by the window. Just to know she was there comforted me.

I lay there with eyes closed, lacerated by grief. Suddenly a great feeling of comfort enfolded me. I felt the presence of David in the room, and it seemed he stood beside the bed. I felt the pressure of his touch as he took my hand, which lay on the cover beside me. He didn't speak, but I sensed he was telling me that everything was going to be all right. His loving presence gave me a peaceful heart as he lingered a few moments, and then he was gone.

I didn't mention this to anyone for quite a while. But weeks later I told my mother, and she surprised me with her reply. She remembered that afternoon in the hospital when she was sitting in the corner chair knitting. She said that she had felt David's presence also. She had stopped knitting, because she didn't want to move and disrupt the moment. She had watched me on the bed and saw my facial expression become serene and knew that I had been comforted. We were both amazed. Had God allowed the veil between this world and eternity to part long enough for me to be comforted in that moment? We believed He had!

God's beautiful healing ministry to me in the hospital was a source of wonder as I pondered on His providential care. God had proven himself true to His Word. As a child, my mother had read the 139th psalm to me many times. The Psalmist David says there is no place we can go that is beyond our Father's care, no place too deep, no place too high, no place too far. He is always there. At only 20 years of age, I had proven it true! Unconscious, afraid, grieving, and so alone, my Lord had come and lovingly cared for me. In His infinite gentleness God was teaching me that He would be in this time of grief, bringing healing and life.

The arrangements for the funeral were being made.

David's body would be shipped from Hannibal to Columbus, Ohio, in order to bury him there near his family. Thankfully my injuries were not as grave as originally feared. I had head injuries, a fractured jaw, and a slight injury to my right eye. My face was swollen and black and blue. I had lost weight because I was on a liquid diet. But I was determined to go to the funeral. I felt that unless I could see David's body and say a final good-bye, I would not be able to comprehend that he was really gone. Dave died early on Saturday morning, but the funeral was delayed until the following Thursday so that I could attend.

The seminary student, Duane,* who had been driving the car we were riding in at the time of the accident, had a severe leg injury and would not be released yet from the hospital. It would be difficult to talk to him, but I wanted to see him. I wanted him to know that I held no bitterness toward him for what had happened. As I considered how to comfort him in the anguish I knew he must be feeling, my thoughts went back to the time when we had begun to plan the trip to see my parents in Peoria, Ill.

My husband, David, was a seminary student in Kansas City. It was August, and he was preparing for his middler year in the coming September. In the spring semester of his first year at seminary, he had been elected to serve as the editor of the *Seminary News,* and he was looking forward to this responsibility. This was one thing he and his friend, Duane, had in common. They both loved to write and had served together on the school paper in college.

David was just finishing a summer school course. We had married in December of his first year in seminary, so we had only been married eight months. He was 22 and I was 20. We were excited about our preparations for the ministry. As a student pastor, he had accepted the pas-

*Not his real name.

torate of a small church in Oregon, Mo. We had a busy schedule. During the day David attended school, and afternoons and evenings he worked at the YMCA. I worked in the Youth Department of the International Headquarters of our denomination as a secretary. One evening a week, I attended the University of Missouri at Kansas City. On the weekends we climbed into our little chromeless Chevy and drove the 90 miles to Oregon, Mo. We called in the community on Saturdays, held a morning and evening service on Sundays, and drove back to Kansas City to be ready for Monday! Still in the honeymoon stage of our life, we dreamed of the ministry we would have together.

David wanted to go to Peoria to see my parents. My father is a minister and at that time was serving in the Illinois area. There was some theological unrest among some of David's friends who were students at the seminary, and he wanted to talk to my father about it. We were going to take a "quick" trip. We would leave Kansas City at midnight, spend all of Saturday with my parents, and travel back to Missouri all night to get to our little church in Oregon for the Sunday services.

I wasn't very excited about taking that kind of a trip and asked David why we couldn't wait until a time when we would be able to spend more time there. He explained that if we would go at that time, we would be able to ride with Duane, as he was going to Chicago and would simply drop us off in Peoria. This would help us financially, so we decided to go.

I didn't feel good about the trip and mentioned several times about delaying it, but David felt a real need to talk to Dad, so we continued our plans.

Before we started out to meet Duane that night, Dave came to the door of our bedroom and told me he was going to go and get some gas in our car. I had been napping before leaving. He asked me to ride with him to the gas station, but I was so tired I didn't want to go. He tried to talk me into it in a teasing way, but I declined. Later, how I wished I had gone!

When he returned, we packed our bags in the car and started off. We were going to drive as far as Cameron, Mo., in our car and leave it there in a church parking lot, and then ride the rest of the way with Duane. It would make it easier for us when we returned and needed to go to Oregon. Just after we had gone a few miles, Dave touched my shoulder and said, "Honey, come over close to me and pray for our trip tonight."

I can remember clearly praying and ending with the phrase, "Lord, if it would be Your will, please give us a safe trip and protect us along the way." This prayer would haunt me later as I tried to deal with Dave's death.

In the early morning hours the three of us stopped at a little roadside cafe for a cup of coffee and a doughnut. When we came out of the store, Dave said, "Carolyn, why don't you get in the backseat and sleep so that when we get to Peoria, at least one of us will be coherent enough to visit with your folks right away."

We had both been sitting in the front with Duane, who was driving, so I slipped into the backseat. But if you knew me, you would know that I like to be where the action is. They were having an animated theological discussion, and I was sitting in the center of the backseat, holding a pillow in my arms and listening intently. They differed in opinion, and I was praying that God would guide Dave's thinking.

The last thing I remember is coming up behind two 18-wheeler tractor trailer trucks. As our friend decided to pass them, I was nervous, because it was raining, and we were going fast on a blacktopped highway. I can remember that after we passed them, I felt a sense of relief. In the early morning darkness, the lights of the truck behind us illuminated the whole inside of our car. I remember no more. The events after that, I learned from others after the accident.

After we passed the two trucks, for some reason, maybe to slow himself down after passing, Duane put his foot on the brake. When he did, the car swerved around on the wet blacktop and crossed into the oncoming lane. A station wagon with eight passengers hit with tremendous impact on the passenger's side of our car. The truck behind us hit us a glancing touch as it struggled to avoid a full impact. It took 45 minutes for an ambulance to arrive. Three people were killed: the driver of the station wagon; a baby held in its mother's arms in the front seat of the wagon; and David.

When I learned the details of what happened, I knew Duane would be blaming himself and suffering for it. Gratefully, I realized I felt no bitterness toward him. God had already begun a healing work in my spirit!

I chose to go and see Duane as I was leaving the hospital. My father took me in a wheelchair to his room. As I entered the room, I could see he had suffered a severe leg injury, and one of his arms had been badly injured also. His face was bruised and swollen. When he saw me, intense emotion was reflected in his eyes as he struggled with tears. I asked him about his injuries, and we talked of mine; but our feelings were so much on the surface it was hard to verbalize what we felt. In halting fashion, I told him that I harbored no bitterness. He was struggling with two emotions: guilt because he was driving when the accident happened, and pain because of the loss of his close friend. I will never forget his last words:

"I only wish it had been me."

On our journey to my parents' home, I lay in the back-seat, trying desperately to remember more of what happened at the time of the accident. But I remembered nothing. Dad felt it would be too traumatic for me to see the cars, and so I was unable to use that experience as a memory trigger point. He did say that Dave's side of the car had taken the greatest impact and that he really hadn't had a chance. If the car in which we were traveling had not been such a good, heavy car, he said, none of us would have survived. As we talked together, we wondered: If the ambulance had arrived sooner, could Dave have lived? Dad had been unable to talk to witnesses at the scene, but we had learned he had not died instantly. Had he responded to anyone? Did he know he was dying? What about those who survived in the other car? How seriously had they been injured?

These uncertainties led to other questions: Why had my life been spared? Dave was the one who was going to preach. He was the tremendous writer. His was the ministry around which our lives were focused! He had such a gift of communication; my goals in life had been wrapped around his. "O God," I echoed Duane in my aching heart. "It should have been me."

As I pondered my own brush with eternity, I became overwhelmed with the actuality of standing before God. He is a holy God, a God of love and mercy, a God of justice. He was the One to whom I had gone for forgiveness of my sins, and I knew He had forgiven me. Now I had the assurance of a redeemed relationship with Him; yet, the thought of how close I had come to stepping through the door of eternity into His presence filled me with trepidation.

I searched my heart and faced the truth that I had not grown in my relationship with the Lord as I could have. Dave had experienced a wonderful time of spiritual renewal and commitment a few months before he died. But I had depended on his strong faith, his spiritual leadership and vitality, and his prayer life to provide the sustenance for my own faith! I hadn't nurtured my own relationship with God. I had been so wrapped up with Dave and our ministry and the goals we were working toward that when he was gone, the depths of my own spiritual foundation were penetratingly revealed.

On the journey to my parents' home I came to the painful realization that where Dave had been gloriously ready to stand before Jesus, I was not ready. I did not want to be less than He dreamed for me. I believe God has a plan and mission for each person. He dreams beautiful possibilities for us and gives us talents and spiritual gifts to enable us to fulfill that plan. But He expects us to walk in intimate relationship with Him, learning to *know* Him personally, so that He can reveal His will to us.

God did not condemn me in those heart-wrenching moments. He created a deep, burning hunger in my heart! From my innermost being I prayed. It wasn't a formal prayer; that wasn't possible—I was too full of pain to put long sentences together. But in disjointed sentences and emotionally laden pauses I bared my soul to Him. I asked His forgiveness for my lukewarm heart, for being willing to live vicariously through the faith of another, instead of continuing to forge my own path with Him. I acknowledged my own helplessness to be other than I was without Him—and He heard my prayer. I was overwhelmed by the Lord's tenderness and gentle encouragement as I faced my need.

I was so moved by this experience that as Dad supported me and I walked into their home, I saw my sister Jeanne and simply said to her, "I was not ready. I was not ready."

As all around me my family prepared for the journey to Columbus, I could only remain in bed. The medication I took for the pain of my head injury made me sleepy. But Jesus understood my grief and loneliness. His presence was with me in that bedroom. Gently He said, "I'm here. I love you. I'll take you from where you are right now and lead you every step of the way. You will never be alone. I'll give you the faith you need and empower you to be all that I have in mind for you to be."

From that day, Jesus became my closest confidant. He began to lead me in an intimacy with Him I had never known before. I could talk to Him, for He understood me in a way no one else could. He accepted me as I was. He knew my strengths and weaknesses. He knew the places where I struggled. He did not condemn me when I poured out my questions or shared my emotional turmoil. He was not threatened. He became my Wonderful Counselor, Mighty God, Everlasting Father, and Prince of Peace!

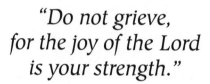

*"Do not grieve,
for the joy of the Lord
is your strength."*

NEH. 8:10

3

Reality's Sting

In this life we will encounter hurts
and trials that we will not be able to
change; we are just going to have to
allow them to change us.[1]   RON LEE DAVIS

Even as I dealt with my grief, it still didn't seem real.
Dave's death had been so sudden. Almost from the time I
had been told, I had felt that unless I attended the funeral,
I would not grasp the finality of it all.

The journey to Columbus was interrupted only once.
We pulled into the parking lot of a motel in Indiana to
spend the night. I was lying in the backseat, but when
Dad stopped the car, I sat up to see where we were. "Dad,
we can't stay here," I cried. "Dave and I stayed in this motel one night on our honeymoon. Please, I can't go in!"

As I looked at the gray-bricked building, I remembered
the night. We were married the week before Christmas,
and we had traveled slowly to Columbus to spend the last
part of the holiday with Dave's family.

On a beautiful, snowy night we had stopped at this
motel to stay. After depositing our bags in the room, we
decided to walk through the snow to the little restaurant
across the street from the motel. Light snow was falling,

and nearly five inches were already on the ground. The restaurant was nearly empty, and we had such fun talking and laughing. When we started back across the street, it had stopped snowing, and the sky was clear. A million stars shone down on us. God seemed so near in the quiet stillness of the night. We were in love and so blessed in that moment!

Now Dave was gone. It was the beginning of many such moments—moments you are never prepared for. Suddenly, you are in a situation that triggers your heart's memories, and you plunge into an intense awareness of your grief all over again. As I would do many times in the future, I tried not to fall apart. In my inner heart I cried out for God's help, His comfort, in that wrenching moment. I didn't want to make it harder for my folks. They loved Dave and were hurting deeply too.

When we arrived in Columbus, I asked to go immediately to the funeral home. David's funeral was the next day, and there would be viewing hours that night, but I needed to be alone to see his body for the first time. My father didn't think I was physically strong enough to go by myself, and so he accompanied me.

As I entered the room at the mortuary, my heart pounded. When I saw David's body, the reality of his death ripped through me. He was gone. I reached out my hand and touched his hand. He would never hold me in his arms again. He would never smile that mischievous sideways grin of his and tease me with gentle relentlessness. We would never again sit and talk for hours, enjoying the way the other's mind operated, learning to know each other.

Dad and I cried together, talking about Dave's injuries and then not talking at all—each alone, letting our grief and love flow through us.

The day of the funeral I was aware of all that was happening; but because of the medication I was taking for my injuries, it seemed as if there were a protective shield around me. I could see and hear, but the pain was blessedly numbed.

Many of Dave's close friends had traveled long distances to be there. As I watched them trying to deal with their grief, it tore at my heart. When the service was over and the final moments arrived, the unshakable reality of the moment pierced through the protective shield. Life would never be the same. Once again I felt deep emptiness and grief.

We returned to David's parents' home. When we entered the living room, there were many family friends there. I was so weary, they urged me to go to an upstairs bedroom and rest. When I was alone in the bedroom, I threw myself facedown across the bed and cried.

From the depths of my lonely heart I cried out to God and said, "O God, what am I going to do now?" Such a simple prayer, not very profound.

For the first and what has been the only time in my life, I heard the audible voice of the Lord. It seemed to come from my right, and I turned that direction when I heard it. I saw no one, but the Voice quietly said, "Go back to school."

An unspeakable peace came over me. I knew what I was to do. Jesus had met me at the point of my need. He knew I had come to the end of my own inner resources. In the midst of pain, despair, and confusion, He brought peace. I went quickly to sleep for the first time since the accident.

When I awoke, I went downstairs. Most of the friends were gone, and it was growing dark. "I know what I am to do now," I told my family. "I am to go back to school!" I was elated because God had revealed himself to me.

My father pointed out that it was August 11, and school started in early September. I was not supposed to travel for two weeks, and then we needed to return to Missouri to pick up my car and our things. It might be too late to apply for entrance. Would the college want me to live in a dormitory, and who could I get for a roommate this late?

In reply to his concerns, I told them about my experience with the Lord as I had cried out to Him in prayer. We all decided that if God had spoken, He would work out all the details. Dad would start the process of inquiry while I stayed with Dave's parents until I was able to travel.

Dad contacted the college I had attended before marrying Dave. The administration worked with him and found a friend of mine who was available to room with me. I would begin school in September!

Now all I had to do was to rest and let my body heal as I waited for the time I could travel. Oftentimes during those days, Dave's family and I looked at old photographs and reminisced. It helped all of us to talk about Dave. I was the last one to be with him before his death, and we needed each other.

Soon the time came to go back to Kansas City. On the trip I learned another lesson about God's sufficiency. We stopped at a motel and went to bed immediately, tired from the hours in the car. But I could not sleep; in fact, I felt myself becoming very agitated. I was exhausted, yet I battled indescribable emotions. Finally, I realized that what was bothering me was the sound of the motor on the window air conditioner. As my parents and I talked about my anxiety, we felt the motor reminded me of the 18-wheeler trucks involved in the accident. We had learned the drivers had left the motors idling at the accident scene. Subconsciously, I remembered and relived the trauma. We prayed, asking the Lord to quiet my emotions and rest my spirit. I was learning to trust Him for every need. Gradually I slept.

The next day we stopped in Cameron, Mo., at the church where Dave and I had parked our car. It sat in the same place, covered with a two-and-a-half-week coat of dust. No one had touched it since we had left it. I wanted to be the first one to touch it now. As I got in the car, a lump rose in my throat. Dave had been excited about getting this new car. It was chromeless with a stick shift and only a few options, but it was ours! I drove the car the rest of the way to Kansas City. It was something of Dave's that I could have with me all the time. It was something that he had provided for me.

In Kansas City we had several stops to make—closing our accounts at the bank, picking up a glossy Dave had ordered for speaking engagements, meeting with a lawyer about legal matters, packing our belongings.

As we finished each task, I knew I was closing a door on that chapter of my life. The finality of it hit me everywhere I turned. At times, my grief was so intense, I would have to find some quiet place alone, a place where I could pour out my tears and heartache to Jesus. I needed the sense of His presence to go on, and each time He comforted me with His peace.

One particular incident seems to best illustrate my feelings. On the trip back to my parents' home we stopped at a restaurant. I was self-conscious, because my face was still bruised and discolored. As quickly as possible, I sat down. After we had ordered, I looked around the restaurant at the people gathered there. When I had entered the restaurant, some had stared at my face; but now they were quietly conversing and carrying on with the details of their lives. It had seemed for just one moment they had acknowledged the trauma of my life and shared it with me. But now it was forgotten.

"How can you people sit there and so nonchalantly go on with the dailiness of your lives?" I wanted to shout! "Don't you realize what has happened? My husband is dead! He'll never know the stages of life you take so much for granted. Can't you feel my pain? Don't you know my life will never be the same again? For one moment there it seemed you were aware, but now . . ."

That's when it hurts so badly—when everyone picks up the pattern of their lives, and there is no pattern to yours at all!

When we arrived in Peoria, my world was shaken once again. My father had received a phone call from David's insurance agent. The agent asked if we knew that the insurance company had received the death certificate and already paid the claim for the policy. Because the cause of death was accidental, a double indemnity had been paid. The payment had been claimed by and paid to Dave's parents.

Upon hearing the news, my mind flashed back to an evening about two weeks before Dave's death. He was working at his desk and called me over to discuss our finances. He showed me insurance forms for a life insurance policy he'd purchased while he was a student in college. The beneficiaries were his parents, but he was filling out a new form, making me the beneficiary. He pointed out the death benefit and the double indemnity clause. Then he told me that his parents had carried two small insurance policies on him also from the time of his birth and that he knew if anything happened to him, they would want me to have the money. Dave went on to explain the financing of our car. He had been paying double payments, and he was excited because God was enabling him to pay it off earlier. He told me about the glossy photo he'd had taken and when it would be ready. "The only other bill we have is for a couple of suits in the cleaners," he said. He concluded by telling me how much money was in our checking and savings accounts at the bank.

I was disturbed that he was being so specific about this, and I told him so. He explained that he didn't want me to worry about how I would make it if something happened to him. "Honey, if something should happen to me," he said, "I want you to finish your education."

At the time of the conversation Dave was 22 and I was 20. I wondered after Dave's death if he had a premonition that he should get those papers done and explain our affairs. But Dave hadn't sent the new beneficiary insurance forms in before the accident, although the agent knew about them because Dave had requested them from him. The agent called my father to let me know what had happened, as he knew Dave's intent.

My father spoke to Dave's father, who confirmed that they had claimed the insurance money. He felt that Dave wanted them to have it because they had raised him, and he had only been married to me for eight months. They felt entitled to keep it. I was devastated. This was the money that would pay for my education.

I can tell you that a picture of the moment I heard that news hangs on the corridor of my mind. The room in which I sat had soft shadows of late afternoon crisscrossing on the pale gray carpet. Sheer curtains swaying in the slight summer breeze brushed the top of the sofa beneath them. I sat in a large, overstuffed chair facing the sofa and windows. The front hall foyer was bathed in light from the open front door. My mother stood just inside the large opening between the living room and foyer, a look of sadness clouding her face as she told me the news. It seemed time stood still as I absorbed the impact of it all.

I can remember that suddenly it seemed as though I was brought acutely aware of the presence of God saturating that room. It was as though He was there waiting for me to be conscious of His presence. He'd been there all the time, ready to meet my need. I wasn't alone. I wasn't powerless. I wasn't without resources. I did not need to be afraid of the future. He was already there. In that instant, when resentment and bitterness were digging their way to take root in my heart, I cried out to God. Desperately I told Him I couldn't handle anything more.

I knew the wishes of Dave's heart. He had talked to me and perhaps unknowingly prepared me for this moment. He loved his parents deeply and would not want a rift between us. I could not allow that to happen in honor of him. But only God could uproot the seed of bitterness struggling to bury itself in the soil of my soul. In that moment God worked a miracle and snatched it away! The inner battle had been so intense, I was emotionally drained. But He brought peace.

Oftentimes in the years since, I have struggled with these same feelings in other situations. I have wanted God to heal me instantly just as He did in this situation. But God does not always heal instantly. Sometimes the healing comes just as surely, but slowly, as He works His healing balm on our lives. But He *does* heal!

In the quietness of my parents' home I confessed my inadequacy to bring healing in this situation. I asked God for wisdom. I reminded Him of how often I had spoken when I should have been silent, how I had not always said the healing thing in threatening situations. I had retaliated with quick words. I surrendered my tongue and my mind to Him, *knowing* I would fail unless His power and love was able to freely flow through me.

I tried to see the situation from Dave's parents' point of view. They were nearing retirement and were probably anxious about their finances. Second, their life focus had been on Dave's ministry and dreams for his future. This money was their last link with their son. Extreme stress or trauma can make any of us respond in ways that are not normal to our personality. I believe this was the case with Dave's father. He was not the same man after Dave died. He had always been a kind man, respected and loved by his children. This was *not* a normal reaction for him. His grief caused him to react in other areas of life as well, behaving in ways not consistent with his personality.

I have learned that in crisis times we cannot program how another person will react, or how long it will take him to deal with the emotions brought on by the crisis. We seem to have special difficulty with family members we have felt we knew so well. It is easier to have greater toleration for others outside the family.

At the time the trauma takes place, our loved ones are already dealing with other circumstances in their lives. This is just one more thing, and so our response to the trauma is colored by the hues of all these emotions.

It is helpful to be sensitive to the dynamics in these situations. We should be careful what we say and do. Because of our own intense emotions, the logical counterbalance in our minds may not be heard as loudly as it should be. As a result we are apt to retaliate. Oh, how we need to *cling* to God in times like these. Satan would rob us of peace and harmony and the quiet joy that comes from appropriating the power and presence of our Lord! But God *will* defeat his efforts if by faith we lean on Him.

Asking God to help me choose the timing and to prepare their hearts for my request, I called Dave's parents and asked them if they would loan me half of the money they received from the insurance company to help me pay for my education. I told them I would pay them back on a regular basis as quickly as I was able. They agreed to the loan, and I was grateful—for I had an emotional attachment to its link with Dave. It was that money he had talked about as a provision for my education, and now it would be so. Dave's brothers and sister were grieved by the situation as well, and we were grateful God's love prevailed.

In the following years Dave's family and I worked diligently to keep our relationship one of love and caring. I drove from school in Illinois to see them in Ohio for weekends. They came to the school to share with me in some of the special moments in my life. Our love for each other deepened during those years. The loan never had to be repaid. That picture in the corridor of my mind has lost its power to ravage me. The sting is gone!

David's father died within a few years, still carrying a deep sense of grief for his son. Later, David's mother died. She called me from the hospital to tell me she was very ill. In a voice so faint I could hardly hear it, she told me she could not love me any more if I had been her own child.

At her funeral, as I sat with the family, I was filled with awe and wonder at the way in which God had answered my prayer that day in my parents' home. I had no regrets and no "if onlys" because of the mighty power of a merciful God who is in the healing business. His desire is to heal the hurts of each of us in a far greater measure than we could ask or think!

"May the God of hope fill you with all joy and peace as you trust in him, so that you may overflow with hope by the power of the Holy Spirit."

ROM. 15:13

4

Second Time Around

We never learn anything new about God
except in adversity.   WATCHMAN NEE

I rounded the curve of the road leading to the main entrance of the campus. Slipping into second gear, I turned
into the drive. As the car moved up the slight grade, I
glanced at the gray-stoned administration building to my
right. The broad, flat steps that circled the front of the
building up to the center door were filled with students en-
thusiastically greeting one another. I smiled. It was all so
familiar. Slowly I drove around the circle, past the boys'
dorm, Chapman Hall, and turning right drove a little further down to Williams Hall, the girls' dorm. I pulled into a
parking space beside the dorm.

I sat there in the car for just a moment, a little reluc-
tant to get out and greet anyone. My heart was filled with
emotion. Everywhere I looked—all the well-loved land-
marks—were clothed with memories of significant moments with Dave. Turning in my seat a little, I could see
the big tree Dave had leaned against the day he introduced himself to me. Looking the other way, I could see
all the places we had walked by the hour.

Tears stung my eyelids as still-raw grief tore at my

heart. How could I stand to be here without him? But even in the pain I knew this was where I was to be. God had led me here.

As I sat, I recalled the thoughts I'd shared with God en route earlier that day. I had only been away a year. Many of the mutual friends Dave and I had known were still here. It would be difficult to see them at first. I knew it would be hard for them also. I had asked God to help me hold myself together when I was with my friends and in public situations during this year. I prayed that I would not grieve publicly, that somehow I would be able to find private places to do that. I did not want people always to be thinking of my situation, making it awkward for them and hard for me to blend into campus life. I wanted this year to be an oasis of healing. In silent entreaty, I had asked God for eyes to see Him in the shadows, for faith to reach out to Him, and for openness to His love.

I got out of the car to go register, making a conscious choice to believe He had heard my prayer and would help me.

This was my second time around as a student on this campus. As I approached the dorm, I thought of the first time I had come. Inwardly I smiled as I remembered how I had carefully chosen the red-and-white dress I would wear that first day. I had wanted to make a good first impression. I knew my college experience was a significant milestone in my life.

In a sense I felt the same way now that I had then. This time at school would be as pivotal a time in my personal maturity as then. I would once again be trying to find a new understanding of my own personal identity. Then I was struggling to mature as an 18-year-old. Now I was struggling to deal with cataclysmic change in my life as a young widow. My identity needed to be redefined. I needed time to work through the reality of my life. This year of schooling before I needed to make career decisions would give me that.

My relationship with Christ, in the month since the accident, had changed. It had taken on a deeper dimension. I walked with a more intimate awareness of God's presence. I felt His sheltering love, sensed His committed involvement, experienced His power. It gave me a security I had not known before and an inner awareness that even though I didn't know the way ahead, He did.

But it was difficult. My inner resources were fragile. I learned to depend on God, at times literally, moment by moment.

My first few encounters with those who had known Dave were painful, yet comforting. They wanted to express their sympathy and grief. I wanted to respond appropriately. As we struggled to communicate with one another, we did not always use the right words. Sometimes we had to listen to hearts. I tried not to take offense when people said things like "You're young; you'll remarry again"; or "You were in the honeymoon stage of your marriage; it will be easier to get over than if you had been married a long time." Those kinds of words hurt unbearably, but I tried to keep in mind that people often do not know what to say in the presence of grief, and so they say the wrong thing.

I learned that it is best to use few words and to simply express love. A caring handclasp or comforting hug with the words "I love you and will be praying for you" is sufficient. The effort to explain the reason for the trauma or to offer an easy solution usually is best left unsaid.

As the school year got under way, I began to adjust to a new life-style. The demands of my studies made it necessary for me to concentrate. This was difficult, but I needed something worthwhile to redirect my thinking.

Social relationships were different. What a culture shock to be back in a dorm of all girls! But my roommate and other close friends did their best to try to make the transition easier. They would talk of Dave easily and naturally, because they knew I needed to be able to talk about him. But they also understood when it was necessary for me to get into my little car and be alone. There were times when I would drive toward Chicago and find a little restaurant where I could eat and sit quietly alone, not needing to wear a mask to cover my hurting. At other times I would go to the state park near the school and sit there in my car and cry, letting my grief go. When the emotional storm was over, I was able to go back and pick up my work.

I was not able to consider dating. Dave's death had been so sudden that I still felt married. I could not close this chapter of my life as yet. There was a loneliness within me no one could fill. After the first three or four months, some well-intentioned older people began to subtly suggest I should put my grief behind me. But I knew there were things I had to work through before I would be ready.

One of the things I missed the most since Dave's death was the long conversations we used to enjoy. We were able to talk about everything. He would share his interest in the theological concepts he was learning at school. I would talk of my dreams for the future. We would laugh and tease each other as we enjoyed the uniqueness of each other's personalities.

All this was a part of our eight months together. But now he was gone. I had wished I had a brother I could talk things over with and hear a man's point of view. Our relationship had added richness to my thinking.

I discovered that there are various stages of grief. At first, there was the shock and the denial of it all. I couldn't believe it had actually happened. I tried to pretend it was untrue, to shut out the pain.

For me there was a period I can only describe as the "if onlys" stage. As I thought back to the events preceding the accident, I tortured myself with thoughts such as: Why didn't I insist on waiting to go another time? I had experienced a sense of deep unease about the trip. I had even dreamed the night before we left that Dave had died. I awoke crying heartbrokenly. Dave was concerned. He thought I was crying because I was homesick for my parents. But I couldn't seem to tell him about the dream. Could I have tried harder to change his mind?

I remember I was afraid to trust my feeling as a premonition, because I felt your dreams could be influenced by your own stream of thoughts. I hadn't wanted to go because of the brevity of the trip and traveling all night both ways that it necessitated; and I worried about driving with so little sleep. How much of that had influenced my feelings about it all?

The next step in the grief process seemed to be dealing with anger. It is hard to describe the kind of anger I felt in coming to terms with my grief. It was not a feeling of blame or resentment at any person. Duane had not been intentionally careless, and so I did not blame him. The anger I can remember feeling was simply an anger that accidents happen, that life is interrupted, that the separation is so final!

Somehow I didn't blame God. I didn't ask, "Why me?" After all, why not me? I knew that being a Christian did not isolate you from life's hard places. From the beginning moments in the hospital, His loving, protective presence had been gloriously real to me. Blame and bitterness had not been able to take root where God's healing love was so keenly felt. Even in the midst of pain there was a quiet joy because God was there. Ps. 16:11 says, "You will fill me with joy in your presence." I found it to be true.

I gave myself permission to grieve. I did not want to be morose, but I did want to give my emotions a chance to heal. My grief pulsated with thankfulness that I had been able to love and be loved by a fine man. I cherished the memories of fun and joy, meditated on the ways I had matured as a person because of his influence on my life, staggered at the inexpressible loneliness, and wept at death's awful finality.

Although the stages are similar, the journey through the grieving process will be different for every person. When we enter moments of intense crisis, many factors are at work. We respond to life events in a way that is unique for each one of us, and we bring our total being into the process. What we are shapes our recovery. Several elements shape our personhood:

1. our God-given personality type
2. our family birth order
3. our relationship with the significant others in our lives (mother, father, siblings)
4. the atmosphere of the home in which we grew up
5. our culture (which includes societal and religious influences)
6. our concept of God

I was a minister's daughter and the firstborn of three girls. Before I was seven years old, my father had pastored three churches. He soon became what our church calls a district superintendent, first in New York and then Illinois. As the administrator over many churches, my father traveled and was away from home a good deal of the time.

My mother was a tremendously talented woman. She had a lovely contralto voice, and she played the violin, piano, and vibraharp. Mother was shy, but she had a warm, caring personality. She was a tall, elegant lady with a delicious sense of humor.

Mother was proud of her Scotch ancestry, often using Scottish phrases to spice up her conversation. She suffered from a blood condition in her leg that was a result of my birth. Many times she would have to stay off her feet until an ulcerated area healed. Through her illness she never complained. And never once did she blame me.

Mother could not always travel with Dad because of

this. When we moved to New York, we lived in the Queens area of New York City. It was during World War II, and the city was inundated with servicemen. Air raids were not unusual. The city seemed overwhelming to us. It was a new and different world.

We lived in a second-floor apartment. One night when my father was gone, I awoke and heard my mother crying in their room next door. Feeling a little frightened, I slipped out of bed and into her room. When she realized I was there, she held out her arms to me, and I crawled on-to the bed with her. I asked her why she was crying.

She explained to me that she was not used to being in a big city like this. Also, she was not used to Dad traveling so much, and she was lonely for him. She said that be-cause she was so shy, it was harder for her to make friends, and so she did not yet know many people. But she carefully explained that she knew God would help her ad-just, because it was His will for us to be there. She helped me see that if we would do our best to adjust to our new circumstances, this would help Dad in his ministry. Each member of the family was important in helping the others.

What a beautiful gift Mother gave me that night. She shared her anxiety with me in a positive way, helping me form my basic attitudes toward my father's ministry. Be-cause of her influence I never resented being a minister's daughter.

Because Mother was often forced to remain in bed, the highlight of my day would be to come home from school, hop on her bed, and share the events of the day. Those times with her helped me to form my concept of womanhood. She counseled me and helped me see the uniqueness of my own personality.

Often she read Psalm 139 to me. As she did, I began to see God's love for me. The wonder of the words:

O Lord, you have searched me and you know me.
You know when I sit and when I rise;

> you perceive my thoughts from afar.
> You discern my going out and my lying down;
> > you are familiar with all my ways.
> Before a word is on my tongue
> > you know it completely, O Lord.
> You hem me in—behind and before;
> > you have laid your hand upon me.
> Such knowledge is too wonderful for me,
> > too lofty for me to attain *(vv. 1-6)*.

I had learned many Scripture verses in Sunday School and church, but these times by the side of her bed made the Bible personally applicable to me. She helped me understand that there was within me a need for God's forgiveness. She helped me understand what sin was. It was disobedience to the will of God as revealed in His Word, the Bible. Rom. 3:23 says: "For all have sinned, and come short of the glory of God" (KJV). Each of us has sinned, but God loved us before we were even aware of Him. He has been actively involved in helping us to become open to His love and forgiveness.

These verses in Psalm 139 reveal His caring nature.

> For you created my inmost being;
> > you knit me together in my mother's womb.
> I praise you because I am fearfully and wonderfully made;
> > your works are wonderful, I know that full well.
> My frame was not hidden from you
> > when I was made in the secret place.
> When I was woven together in the depths of the earth,
> > your eyes saw my unformed body.
> All the days ordained for me
> > were written in your book
> > before one of them came to be.
> How precious to me are your thoughts, O God!

How vast is the sum of them!
Were I to count them,
    they would outnumber the grains of sand.
When I awake,
    I am still with you *(vv. 13-18)*.

The awe I felt to think that God was there when I was created in my mother's womb. He *knew* me, and yet, He loved me still! I could not count the number of times each day that His thoughts turned toward me! I was not able to comprehend it. But day by day as I discovered who I was and gradually became aware of my need for God, Mother was leading me in love to see Him.

It was not hard for me to understand the concept of sin. I found myself in trouble a great deal of the time, for I was a strong-willed child. I can remember one day my mother saying to me, "Carolyn, if your will is surrendered to the Lord, there is no telling what wonderful things God will be able to do in your life. But if not, I shudder to think what will happen." I never forgot those words.

I tested every boundary. So I understood what sin was. I remember that finally, Mother was able to help me see that if I was unhappy with the person I was becoming, it only made sense to go back to my Creator. He understood me as no one else would ever understand me. She said that if she had a Sears refrigerator that did not perform the function for which it was created, she would call Sears to come and fix it. If her sewing machine did not work, she would take it to Singer's and ask them to repair it. So if I was unable to become the person I wanted to be, I should go to God, my Creator.

Mother helped me see that God has a dream for every individual person. He gives us talents, personality traits, and character potential to help us fulfill that dream. We need not compare ourselves to anyone else. We need only work toward becoming all that God has in mind for us to be. If we will give our lives to Him, enabling His power to work in us, He will give us spiritual gifts that would enable us to carry out His purpose in our lives. Even more wonderful, He will always be with us. There is no place beyond the shelter of His loving care.

> Where can I go from your Spirit?
> Where can I flee from your presence?
> If I go up to the heavens, you are there;
> > if I make my bed in the depths, you are there.
> If I rise on the wings of the dawn,
> > if I settle on the far side of the sea,
> even there your hand will guide me,
> > your right hand will hold me fast *(Ps. 139:7-10)*.

When I was eight years old, one Sunday morning at a little church in Dover, N.J., at the close of the morning worship service, I prayed and asked Jesus to forgive me of my sin and to help me to be all that He dreamed for me to be. First John 1:9 says: "If we confess our sins, he is faithful and just and will forgive us our sins and purify us from all unrighteousness."

I trusted His promise to forgive me. I don't remember any great feeling coming over me. But when I walked out of that little church I felt clean. And when I looked at my world, it looked like it had been washed clean too. The grass looked greener and the sky looked bluer! God and I began a walk together that day.

This was the beginning. The next step was to learn to walk in intimate relationship with Him, allowing Him to transform my life. In *The Living Bible,* Rom. 5:1-2 describes this moment in our lives:

> So now, since we have been made right in God's sight by faith in his promises, we can have real peace with him because of what Jesus Christ our Lord has done for us. For because of our faith, he has brought us into this place of highest privilege where we now stand, and we confidently and

joyfully look forward to actually becoming all that God has had in mind for us to be.

The next verses describe the process of maturing in our concept of Him.

We can rejoice, too, when we run into problems and trials for we know that they are good for us—they help us learn to be patient. And patience develops strength of character in us and helps us trust God more each time we use it until finally our hope and faith are strong and steady. Then, when that happens, we are able to hold our heads high no matter what happens and know that all is well, for we know how dearly God loves us, and we feel this warm love everywhere within us because God has given us the Holy Spirit to fill our hearts with His love *(vv. 3-5, TLB)*.

This is a beautiful description of the process of living out our faith. Oswald Chambers calls our spiritual growth in grace "cultivating the mind of Christ." Eccles. 3:11 says that God "has . . . set eternity in the hearts of men." He wants to help us look at the whole of life through His eyes. This is a lifelong process! In Phil. 3:10-11 the apostle Paul says: "I want to know Christ and the power of his resurrection and the fellowship of sharing in his sufferings, becoming like him in his death, and so, somehow, to attain to the resurrection from the dead."

I asked the Lord to help me make that my primary desire: to *know* Him. God has always been the Initiator in the relationship between himself and man, and He cares passionately about revealing himself to us. His method for revealing himself is primarily through His Word, the Bible. Though Mother helped me begin to have an understanding of God, I had to learn to seek Him on my own, through the pages of Scripture.

My concept of God was affected not only by my mother's teaching and life but also by the influential role of my father. He was a dedicated minister and administrator; in my growing-up years I never heard him preach a message he did not consistently live.

He is a strong-willed man—and my strong will was bound to come in conflict with his. If there was a difference of opinion between us, it was hard for him to listen to my opinion because he was so thoroughly convinced of his! As a result, it seemed to me that he was being controlling.

My father was usually gone during the day and often in the evenings, but he made a concerted effort to share at least one meal a day with us. Even if he had to travel a distance at night, rather than stay all night away from home, he made the choice to come home, so that he could be there for breakfast with us if at all possible. The reason I was so skinny in my teen years was that I frequently had a confrontation with my father at a mealtime. That was the only time he was there, and I didn't get to eat very much!

Though I might disagree with Dad, I never wanted to hurt his ministry, because I loved him. Mother tried to help me understand him. She told me about his background, about his parents, about the legalistic way he had been brought up. She pointed out the ways in which Dad had made his love for me known. She softened the impact of the differences between us. She was committed to helping two strong-willed people come together!

This all had an impact on me when at the age of 18, I came to the point in my life when I realized my need to totally surrender the control of my life to the Lord. I knew I was not experiencing all that God had for me. There was a hunger in my heart for more of Him. I studied in the New Testament in the Book of John, chapters 14, 15, and 16, where Jesus describes the ministry of the Holy Spirit to the followers of Christ. I read the Book of Acts and the rest of the New Testament, looking to see the difference the coming of the Holy Spirit made in the lives of those who followed Him.

The Bible clearly reveals that the Holy Spirit enters our lives when we confess our sins and begin to live in His salvation, but He wants to be first—to have access to every part of our hearts. We surrender ourselves totally to God and ask Him to be the Master and Lord of our life. Our will is no longer first. His will becomes the center of our being. He is Lord. His presence, His love then fills our being, purifying our hearts by faith; His power enables us to obey Him.

I could see the difference in the men and women of the Bible before and after Pentecost. The Holy Spirit enabled them to be what they were created to be. I wanted that power and that relationship with Him, but it was so hard to surrender my will! Jesus gently began to help me see that my difficulty was in my limited concept of Him. He led me to the verse in 1 John 4:18: "We need have no fear of someone who loves us perfectly" (TLB); "perfect love casts out fear" (NKJV). God's love is so much deeper and wiser and more unconditional than any other love that we have no other comparison to help us understand it. But gradually, I began to understand that I could trust Him. I need not be afraid to surrender.

Finally, at the end of my 18th summer I brokenly and totally surrendered to Him. I whispered a simple prayer, asking Him to cleanse my heart of anything that would prevent His Spirit from feeling at home there. I asked Him to fill me through and through with His Holy Spirit. I put a stake down that day that meant I didn't care how many times I might stumble and fall and rub my nose in the dust, God and I were committed to each other. I would belong to Him. By faith in His Word, I believed He filled me with His Spirit.

At first, I had no great feeling. But as the days went by, I was aware of His love and joy flowing through me in a way I had never known before. I was experiencing life with a new perspective. By surrendering my life to Him, I opened my heart to His healing, sanctifying power that has continued to transform me.

Catherine Marshall, in her book *A Closer Walk*, said:

"Jesus was a joyous man!" We are not invited into a relationship which will take away our fun! But we are asked to "enter into the joy of your Lord" (Matt. 25:21, 23, NKJV). Jesus came to earth, He said, in order "that your joy may be full" (John 15:11, NKJV). Jesus drew men to the Kingdom by promising two things:
1. trouble, hardship, danger
2. joy
By what curious alchemy can He make even danger and hardship seem joyous? He understands things about human nature that we grasp only dimly: few of us are really challenged by the promise of soft living, by an emphasis on me-first, or by a life of easy compromise.[1]

Christ still asks for total, full surrender, and then promises His gift of full, overflowing joy. I found that joy!

After my experience with the Holy Spirit, one of the most dramatic tests of this deeper relationship came as I dealt with the legalistic and judgmental attitudes of some Christians where we lived. A decided emphasis on rules of apparel, hairstyle, etc., created an atmosphere of judgmentalism and disharmony. One's relationship with God was assessed by the outward. It seemed inconsistent that people could put so much emphasis on the outward and at the same time show an inward spirit so lacking in love and Christlikeness. The seeming hypocrisy of it all caused many teenagers to drop out of church, never to return.

My personal crisis came one weekend when I came home from college to see my parents. I had cut and permed my hair. Mother and I went shopping, and somehow we got separated in the aisles of the store. As I was coming back to join Mother, I saw a lady from church come up to Mother and say, "Mrs. Eckley, I just saw

Carolyn, and I can see she has cut her hair; and didn't she get a permanent? I'm sure you are upset. What are you going to do about it?" Her tone of voice was quite cutting.

My mother turned to her and said, "I have every confidence in Carolyn. She loves the Lord, and I know she wouldn't do anything she felt was wrong. She is an adult now and makes her own decisions. I am not going to do anything about it. I believe in her!"

My mother then quietly smiled at the surprised woman and left her to find me. As we talked about it on the way home, Mother said to me, "Carolyn, do you think you did wrong by cutting your hair?" I said, "No, Mother, I don't." Then Mother said, "You come to church with me tomorrow, and just be yourself. These are wonderful people, Carolyn, but they do not realize how their spirit is hurting the cause of Jesus."

We talked a long time together about the importance of having principles to live by, yet at the same time a spirit so full of love that the Holy Spirit is free to work His way in people's lives. The next day, Mother walked into church with me and ushered me right to the second row as usual. She put her arm across the back of my pew in a gesture that seemed to be loving protection. The pastor commented in his sermon that morning, saying if someone was going against the accepted code of dress, no matter whose daughter they were, it was wrong. It hurt for him to publicly mention me, yet because of Mother and God's power helping me choose to give Him any thoughts of bitterness, I was able to get through it.

Many people have shared this bruising with me. But we cannot use our hurts as an excuse to walk away from God. We are not responsible for this spirit of legalism in others, only for our own spirit. We can use this kind of experience to come through to a clearer understanding of our Lord and who He is.

There cannot and should not be a rule for every point

of conduct. But there should be strong biblical principles that each of us believes in that will enable us to come to decisions as to the path we take.

All of these experiences affected my concept of God and were the colors I brought with me to weave the tapestry of my life.

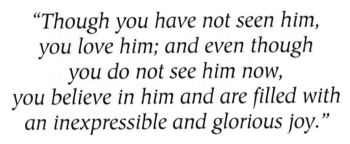

*"Though you have not seen him,
you love him; and even though
you do not see him now,
you believe in him and are filled with
an inexpressible and glorious joy."*

1 PET. 1:8

■III 5

Lonely Horizon

Faith by its very nature must be tried,
and the real trial of faith is not
that we find it difficult to trust God,
but that God's character has to be
cleared in our own minds.[1]   OSWALD CHAMBERS

The sound of my steps reverberated through the empty stairwell as I climbed the metal steps to the second floor of the administration building. It was late afternoon and few classes met at that time of day, so the halls were quiet. Opening the door of the Kelley prayer chapel at the top of the landing, I entered the empty room. Walking around one of the columns spaced about the room, I went to the wall of windows facing south and looked out over the campus.

Early fall. The huge trees across the street from where I stood were blanketed in red and gold. The afternoon sun bathed them in splashes of bright glory. There was a crispness to the cool air that crackled with the promise of football, pep rallies, bonfires, and steamy mugs of hot chocolate. I loved this time of year, and now there was the special excitement of being a senior. Each event would have a unique poignancy that I would savor. I was anxious to graduate, but I knew that my college years had played a pivotal part in my maturing process. There is no other time in your life quite like it.

Since returning to school, I had participated fully in campus life. I was a part of student government, worked on the school newspaper staff, and sang in the Orpheus choir. These activities had been an enriching experience for me. Now as a part of student leadership, I had been asked to speak in chapel to the student body the next day. I was overwhelmed. It is always hard to speak to your peers. Each fall our campus hosted an evangelist, who would hold a week's meetings. In preparation for that time, several students were selected to bring an inspirational talk, sharing our hope for spiritual renewal among the students.

This prayer chapel in which I now stood was the site of meetings for the student prayer band, which met Monday through Friday at 6:15 to 7:00 each evening. I turned from the windows and looked at the room. My mind could hear the music often sung here. I could remember special moments when God had reached down and helped us be aware of His presence in a profound way. It was here that the simple service of a few songs, a brief talk, and testimonies of students gave us food for thought. It was at this altar that confessions had been made, hurts turned over to God, and the direction of lives changed. I had been a part of all of that. I had shed my tears, made my confessions, and reached out to God's healing power.

But now I had to speak in chapel to the whole student body, faculty, and administration. I knew what I wanted to say, but I still wasn't completely comfortable with my message. It needed a touch of fire and passion. My words needed the authority that comes only from knowing that you are saying what God wants you to say. And so I had come to be alone here to meditate, where the echo of other prayers whispered in the walls.

I was struggling in my own faith. Here I was, a person who, in the last year, had enjoyed the protective love of a compassionate Heavenly Father in a way I would never forget. One who had watched God answer prayer after prayer in a miraculous way. I had experienced a peace and joy in spite of a grief more intense than I could articulate. And yet, I was holding onto my faith by what felt like slender threads.

I experienced an unspeakable agony! How could I speak tomorrow with a transparent spirit, declaring faith with surety, when I was plagued by doubt and fear? I knelt down beside a metal folding chair and began to talk to God and to share with Him exactly how I felt.

As I pondered and prayed, I realized that my anguish had begun with my senior year. The safe cocoon of college life would soon be over. My close friends would be building their own lives. We would spread to different areas of the country, each pursuing our own goals. Inevitable change was coming. Once again my life seemed to stretch out to a lonely horizon.

In these circumstances the temptation to doubt that which I had always believed made itself felt. It seemed as if Satan accused me, saying, "Carolyn, you are the most narrow-minded person it has ever been my misfortune to meet. You perceive yourself as becoming a well-educated, professional woman, a person of intelligence and maturity. Yet you have never considered any way of life, any philosophy or any system of belief other than your own. You have believed in God, a personal God who is actively involved in your daily life, a God of love and compassion, an Almighty God with power to enable you to meet the demands of life—but look around you.

"Would a God of love allow your husband to die? Remember how he graduated from college in three years and was trying to finish seminary in two? Why would a caring God do this to Dave when you can see all around you people who are doing absolutely nothing with their lives? Look at the pain you've had! You better rethink what you believe! Can't you see the foolishness of it all? Do you want to spend your life chasing an empty illusion?"

I knelt there talking to God as the questions assailed my mind. And then I was quiet. Spent emotionally. But gradually, a gentle serenity began to settle within me. I had a sense of assurance that God had heard. Just as importantly, I knew He was not angry with my questions nor with my struggles against doubt. God was not threatened by anything I brought before Him. My faith *should* be able to stand up under scrutiny. My belief should not be an unexamined belief.

I thought of the scripture: "Always be prepared to give an answer to everyone who asks you to give the reason for the hope that you have" (1 Pet. 3:15). I knew I wanted to be able to give a clear answer for my faith, but the answer to some of my own questions would have to wait. For now, I knew I did not want to give up the faith I had known. God had revealed himself to me personally many times—I would not deny Him. Eventually I would face the questions that troubled me and work my way through them. But in this moment, I needed to make preparation for the next day. I made a decision to reaffirm to the Lord my desire to keep faith.

I went over the notes for my speech in the quietness of His presence. As I contemplated, thoughts began to come to me that enriched and gave deeper meaning to that which I had written. Soon, I knew I was ready. Instead of being overwhelmed and frightened by tomorrow's task, I began to anticipate it! In wonder I thanked the Lord for removing the debilitating fear of my own inadequacy and for filling me with hope at what He could do in and through me.

The next morning I walked into the auditorium where chapel was held and saw faculty, administration, and students in the audience. For a moment fear washed over me again. But as I sat there in the chair facing the students, God reminded me of His enabling presence the day before and that He often chose inadequate, unqualified, and insignificant people. But *He* had empowered them.

When I stepped to the dark oak pulpit, it was a heartrending moment for me. On its side was a bronze placque, which commemorated it in honor of my husband, Dave. As I gripped the sides of the pulpit and began to speak, I was aware of a sense of personal history.

God taught me so much that day. It was an astounding experience for me. He had so burned the thoughts into my heart and mind that I did not need my notes. I could look into the eyes of my peers, and He enabled me to communicate with them. When I finished, I was in awe of God. Never have I been so humbled as I was that day, when I saw the eyes of the students and knew that God had helped *them* feel what He had enabled me to see!

That experience was a pivotal moment in my life. God was beginning to reveal to me a glimpse of His plans for me. But the way of preparation would be a long one.

The time soon came to deal with the questions that plagued me. Within a few days after my chapel experience, the agony of doubt assailed me again. How does one deal with heart-wrenching temptation? God led me in a very simple way.

The process began as I recalled, as a little girl, listening to the Gideons who would come to our church to make their presentation. I remembered a story they told about a hopeless, inebriated man sitting in a seedy, lonely hotel room. He would notice the Gideon Bible placed on the nightstand, pick it up, and somehow be drawn to read in the Book of John. There by the light of the flickering neon sign outside his window, God would speak to him through that Gospel, and he would learn that God loved him just as he was—in all of his sin. He would learn that if he would confess his sin, his sins would be remembered against him no more. He would be forgiven. Jesus Christ, through His Spirit, would live within him, teaching him the meaning of life from God's perspective.

I said to God: "If a hopeless, inebriated man sitting in a lonely hotel room can, by the light of a flickering neon sign outside his window, read the Book of John and feel You speak personally to him, will You speak to *me* in such a way that as I read the Book of John, I will see You, Jesus, as I have never seen You before, with all the wonder of who You are? I know that You have reached out to me. You have been closer to me than anyone else these last two years. I have known Your comforting presence. I have been aware of Your thoughts flowing through my mind, bringing inconceivable joy in the wrenching moments of my life. But I am torn by questions, Lord, that can only be answered if I seek You." In brokenness I cried, "Help me, Lord!"

During the next two months, each day I tried to find some time to read the Book of John. Sometimes it was late at night before I was able to be alone. The senior girls lived in some small ranch-style homes that had been converted for the use of eight girls and a resident counselor. The rooms were small, and privacy was scarce. Many times I had to slip into the bathroom after everyone had gone to bed, to find light so that I could read without disturbing anyone's sleep. But I was determined.

Before I would begin to read, I would bow my head and remind the Lord of my need, and ask Him to reveal himself to me. I will never forget the first night: "In the beginning was the Word, and the Word was with God, and the Word was God. The same was in the beginning with God. All things were made by him; and without him was not any thing made that was made. In him was life; and the life was the light of men. And the light shineth in darkness; and the darkness comprehended it not" (John 1:1-5, KJV).

The concept of God that I saw in just those beginning verses gripped me. I stopped reading. The profound significance of this truth overwhelmed me. I grasped the certainty that *my concept of God was the most important reality in my life.* It would shape me, guide me, and motivate me in all aspects of my life and character. The verses throb with the intensity of certitude as John witnesses. He had walked with Jesus, talked with Him, suffered with Him, and cried with Him, and he declared: "He is who He claimed to be. He is God!"

If I want to know the character of God, I must, as John did, look at Jesus, for He is the Revelation of God to us. As I read, God revealed himself to me in interesting ways. Sometimes I was able to read only a few verses before I had to stop and ponder what I had read. The words of the Scripture seemed to leap from the pages with life and vibrancy. It was as though I was sitting on the dusty desert floor listening to the thundering words of John the Baptist—a man whose whole life was dedicated to simply preparing the way for Jesus.

I watched the way Jesus interacted with the men who began to follow Him and later became His disciples. I tramped the stony pathways with the sand filtering through my shoes as I listened to the conversations Jesus had as He walked. I sat on the side of the hill beside the lake as Jesus taught from a boat. I sensed the authority in His voice and compassion in His expression as He shared His love with those who listened.

Occasionally I would read two or three chapters at a time, the narrative in its entirety splashing its vivid color and depth across the canvas of my mind. Many pictures, never to be forgotten, etched their spiritual beauty in my heart.

Certain verses I would read slowly and then reread,

word by word, intensely trying to see the truth Jesus was seeking to reveal. That's when I knew I would spend a lifetime learning to know Him. I began to understand Isa. 55:8-9: "'For my thoughts are not your thoughts, neither are your ways my ways,' declares the Lord. 'As the heavens are higher than the earth, so are my ways higher than your ways and my thoughts than your thoughts.'"

When I read the 20th chapter of John, verses 30 and 31 were indelibly engraved on my heart and mind. "And many other signs truly did Jesus in the presence of his disciples, which are not written in this book:

"But these are written, that ye might believe that Jesus is the Christ, the Son of God; and that believing ye might have life through his name" (KJV).

I closed my Bible. Tears began to cascade down my face. A deep, inner certainty spread throughout my being. I knew God was there. I sat in silence, feeling as though speaking aloud would shatter the moment. But then gradually, in the sweet presence of the Holy Spirit, I quietly spoke to the Lord, reaffirming my belief in Him.

After this encounter with God through His Word, I realized that life is a continual interaction between ourselves and God. Each day opens up new dialogue, new revelation, new understanding; we never "arrive." Life is too complex for that. The depths of God are rich, and we are poor. We may be tripped up by the bruising events of our lives. But God will teach us how to stretch beyond the broken image we have of ourselves to the image of possibility that He has of us.

As I began to walk in ever-deepening relationship with Him, I realized how small my image of Him was. At times this limited His ability to minister to me. Often I would have to fight my despair at my own stumbling. But He didn't condemn me. As I studied Scripture, I saw that although Jesus did not trust human nature, He was not cynical about it. He knew what the power of God could do in the life of someone totally committed to Him. He is always there for us in gentle mercy, waiting to show us more of himself!

I found I *enjoyed* God! I learned that He would laugh with me as well as weep with me. God loved me, so in the safety of that love, I could share everything with Him. He and I chuckled together over some of the hilarious things of life. And sometimes, even in difficult times I discovered little moments where God and I would smile together.

One of those times came when just after Christmas break, I had to go back to Missouri for the trial concerning the accident in which David had been killed. The widow of the man in the other car was suing the driver of our car, Dave and me, and the trucking company of the two semi-trailers involved.

I had had some unpleasant moments when her lawyers had come to see me at school and tried to talk to me without the benefit of having my lawyers there. I refused to talk to them. They did not believe that I did not remember anything about the actual accident itself. They were hoping to trick me into making statements that would reveal that I actually remembered but was refusing to tell. But at that time, I remembered nothing. (To this day, I have remembered only one small part of the scene, and that came to me in later years.)

When the time for the actual trial began, I was fearful, as I had never testified in court. I realized that I had to be alert and measure my words carefully. My heart went out to the widow whose husband and baby had died. But I felt her lawyers were not conducting themselves in her best interests. As I expected, the lawyer tried to tear apart my testimony and my character. But I could only tell the truth. I had no memory of the accident from the time up to the actual impact to waking up in the hospital hours later.

But evidence in the trial included pictures of the scene of the accident. These revealed every detail. It was painful. But just before the trial session one day, a man walked up to me and introduced himself to me as the truck driver of one of the trucks involved. He said that he had come to the trial as a witness for the trucking company, but he had also come for another reason. He wanted to talk to me. He told me this story.

After the accident, which involved a station wagon, two 18-wheeler tractor trailer trucks, and our car, it took almost 45 minutes for an ambulance to arrive. While the truck driver and others were waiting, they had managed to get the door open on the passenger side of our car so that they could reach in to try and help us. They did not know I was in the car because the front seat had been pushed into the backseat, and I was covered up with it. But they saw Dave painfully trying to turn around in the seat and talk to me. Dave was gravely injured, and yet he was concerned more about me than his own condition. He talked to me quietly and haltingly for quite a while. Gradually, his head fell back, and he was quiet.

When the ambulance finally arrived, they cared for Dave, who was the most seriously injured, first. After he was examined, the ambulance attendant pronounced him dead and walked away. The truck driver was standing by Dave's side, and he turned to his partner and asked him to get a sheet out of the truck to cover Dave. He turned around to our car again to look inside, and Dave opened his eyes and in a voice that could hardly be heard, asked, "Will everyone be all right?" The driver was so shocked he didn't remember what he answered. But he said then Dave died without responding again.

As the truck driver recounted this story, I was amazed. I had no remembrance of any of it. I said, "Do you mean that after they pronounced him dead, he spoke?" And he said, "Yes!" We could not help but smile at the picture of the driver's face as it must have been in that moment. I smiled, too, because even in death Dave's attitude had been a witness for the Lord.

The truck driver continued: "The reason I wanted to talk to you is that I have chosen to be a character witness for your husband. Any man that is more concerned for others than himself at the moment of death has to be a man of fine character. I watched his actions and spoke to him, and I want you to know that his personal integrity shone through even in his last moments."

After the trial, I returned to school. The affirming of my faith through reading the Book of John, and the knowledge of God's presence with me during that time, enabled me to learn other ways to effectively deal with doubt. I found that:

1. When struggling with a concept of faith, I must keep my mind as open to the concepts of God's truth as I am to considering any other philosophy! Satan would like us to throw aside all that we have learned and label it as spurious and intellectually inferior. But since what we believe shapes our whole destiny, we must be careful. If we have chosen to follow Jesus, we ought to seek counselors who know His Word and are spiritually mature.

2. I must remember, as the children of Israel were cautioned to do in the Book of Joshua, to keep before my mind the precious experience I have had of intimate relationship with Christ and the personal knowledge of living in His presence. He had been my closest friend and had answered my every need during this crisis time in my life. No one could take that away from me!

3. When it comes to the basic decisions of life, it is necessary to think honestly as you consider the options. There is a risk, no matter which path you choose.

Living for Christ is risky. No one can indisputably prove the existence of God. Living for Christ is daring to believe there is a God, and living life consistent with that belief, with all of its benefits for this life and in eternity. It is knowing that suffering may come, even though you believe. It is knowing that you will be involved in the battle of the ages, aligned with God and all His mighty power. It is knowing that to live life as Christ would want us to live cannot be done in our own strength or power. It is choosing to live, believing God will give us power to live beyond ourselves.

There is also the option of choosing to live life without God. I believe this is the greater risk. You may find achievement and happiness through belief in your own personal strength or through causes that are bigger than yourself. You may be successful in a productive career and enjoy a deep, fulfilling love with someone. But there is still the possibility that to give real ethical meaning to one's life, to integrate one's public and private selves to one emphatic statement for integrity, is impossible without the higher power of God. It is knowing the risk of choosing to live life believing there is no eternity that one must face.

We all must take the risk—one way or the other. We are responsible for our own personal destiny. We make the choices. No matter what life has thrown at us. No matter where we are in our journey. We have chosen to live life in a certain way. How have you chosen?

If we choose to follow Jesus, we enter a relationship with God in which we have the privilege of learning to know Him better every day. We can rip away the erroneous remnants of limited understanding about Him and replace them with radiant garments of spiritual perception. If we should turn out to be wrong, we have lost only some temporary pleasures. But if we are right, we have gained power to live to the utmost His dream when He created us. We have placed ourselves within His healing power, spiritually and emotionally and physically. And we have gained the hope of forgiveness of sin and a glorious eternity with Him.

If we choose to reject God, we have gained temporary

pleasures. We have made ourselves the source of all our hope. We have missed knowing the God who created us and loves us with a love we will never receive from any other person. And our life here on earth becomes the end in all. Would this perhaps give us a glimpse into the hell of eternity?

In *World Vision* magazine, Charles Mayes said: "Make sure the thing you are living for is worth dying for."

"But let all who take refuge in you be glad; let them ever sing for joy. Spread your protection over them that those who love your name may rejoice in you."

PS. 5:11

To Live Again

Those who believe they believe in God
but without passion in the heart,
without anguish of mind, without uncertainty,
without doubt, and even at times without despair,
believe only in the idea of God,
and not in God himself.   UNAMUNO

It takes a tremendous amount of relationship to God for a
man to BE what he is."   OSWALD CHAMBERS

Nearly everything I owned was in my little chromeless
green Chevy as I cruised down Paseo Boulevard in Kansas
City. The car was so tightly packed there was only room
for me to sit and drive. My ironing board rested on top of
boxes and over the seat, carefully keeping everything level
so that I could see out the rearview mirror. I carefully
watched for the street where the school was in which I
would teach. When I found it, I quickly turned to the right
and drove slowly by the older brick building. This was the
start of my career!

With diploma in hand, which signaled I had completed the B.S. in elementary education, I had decided to return to Kansas City to teach. I had found a second-floor

apartment in a lovely home on Virginia Avenue. It was a short distance from there to the church I had chosen to attend. Everything was in place for a new chapter in my life. As I turned back onto Paseo Boulevard, I continued south. Soon I crossed 63rd Street and drove around the curve where I could see the seminary Dave had attended. Though I was saddened by the memories, I was also excited about a new beginning.

I began teaching third grade. I had 33 students, with nearly an even mixture of black and white students. How quickly I faced my own inadequacy. I discovered that without realizing it, I had accepted racial stereotypes in my thinking. My experiences in interacting with blacks was limited, but what relationships I had had were positive and meaningful. In the classroom, though, I discerned there was a lack of expectation in my approach to the black children. I tended to put labels on them too quickly. It scared me when I realized that this tendency that I had not appreciated in others was one I shared!

I realized how shallow my thinking was and knew I needed help. Firmly believing that God had opened the door for me to teach here, I desperately sought His help.

Several ideas came to mind as I opened my thinking to Him.

1. I determined to arrive at school at least a half hour before the other teachers. I would take that time to pray for each student in my class by walking up and down the aisles and pausing at each desk. I would visualize each child and ask God to help me see him or her as He saw them. I asked Him to help me dream His dreams for that child's life.

2. I prayed that His Spirit would so permeate that classroom that there would be a feeling of safety and love for all of us as we entered that room.

3. I asked for wisdom and a willingness to be taught, for an openness with the black teachers.

4. I asked God to strip away from my heart any preconceived ideas that would limit my effectiveness.

5. I determined to learn as much about the black culture as I could so that I could better appreciate and encourage my students' heritage.

Little did I realize the stretching and growing and inward pain I would experience in answer to that prayer. I saw myself as I was, and I did not like what I saw! I thought that I was a much more "enlightened" person than that! But God began to change me. He incisively stripped away the erroneous in my thinking and replaced it with better understanding and love. As I daily prayed the above prayer, I saw God begin to answer in gentle ways. Each child began to take on a unique personality and potential. I searched for ways to know them better so that I could help them feel special and good about themselves. What were the results?

1. God helped me see that it was vitally important to create a positive atmosphere of hope, because so much in these children's lives was negative and hopeless. What creative ideas the Lord gave me! I used music, creative drama, affirmation, and sheer enjoyment of the things that made them unique.

As the children began to feel safe with me and believe that I was *for* them, they began to teach me about the ways in which we were different and the commonalities we shared. For instance, the black children talked to me about their skin and how they had to care for it. One little boy named Thomas lifted his pant leg to his knee one day and showed me his skin. It was almost gray and flaky. He said, "You see, Mrs. Miller, we have to put oil on our skin, or it gets like this. I forgot to do it!" We chuckled together. But then I showed him how my skin, especially at the elbows, would get flaky and rough if I did not use lotion also!

The children participated in my life. When they found

out that I was a widow, they took it on as their personal responsibility to find me a man. When a man who was single would walk into our room, they would giggle and whisper, hoping this might be the one! One little boy, whose name was James, came up one morning and said, "Mrs. Miller, I heard a song about you last night."

"Oh, really, James," I said. "What was the song?"

Slapping his thigh with his hand in delight, he said, "The Merry Widow Waltz!" How we laughed!

2. These children knew more about life at their age than I did at the same age. The harsh realities of life were a daily fact. I came to see how some had been brought up with a victim mentality and a hopelessness that was frightening in its intensity. But there were others (and it was interesting to see that most of these had some kind of religious upbringing) who had a desire and determination to succeed no matter what the limitations of their circumstances. I needed the counseling of the black teachers there to learn how to motivate those who felt victimized and hopeless. There are no easy answers for injustice. Laws can only do so much. They do not change the heart of a person.

There were many times after the children left for the day that I had to spend a few quiet moments alone. The more I had learned about their lives, the heavier the burden I felt for them became, and I could not carry it alone without feeling helpless. Only God could give me hope again.

My second year at this school was a disaster. I asked to teach fourth grade in a room across the hall from my room. It was a larger room. I did not factor in the reality that a larger room would mean an increase in the number of students. That second year I had 45 students and no helper!

It seemed to be an impossible situation. I felt fortunate if I was able to teach anything at all, because discipline was such a factor. I was so busy trying to create an atmosphere in which one could learn that the effort nearly wore me out.

Midyear I asked to resign. But the supervisor talked me into staying and said they would give me a classroom with a smaller number of students the next year. Many days I would cry all the way home, feeling as though I was failing the children's emotional needs, failing as a professional teacher, and failing as a representative of Jesus.

I remembered something Oswald Chambers wrote in *My Utmost for His Highest*:

"It is one thing to go through a crisis grandly, and another thing to go through every day glorifying God when nobody is paying any attention to you."[1]

Ouch! As I opened myself to the Lord, He showed me that the lenses of my mind had been so shuttered with the enormity of my problem, He could not enable me to picture His solution. He taught me to depend totally on Him and to take one day at a time. I will confess that one of my favorite verses became: "And it came to pass." Thankfully, it did!

One of the things that deeply distressed me as I was teaching was to see the emotional pain so many of these young children knew. There grew within me a desire to help them in a more direct way in these areas of their lives. I decided to begin a graduate program in guidance and counseling that would enable me to be an elementary school counselor. I decided to attend the University of Oregon for the summer session where I could further my education, enjoy new scenery, and have the adventure of meeting new people.

The Sunday before I left for Oregon, I was walking down the hall of my church when I saw a young man leaning down to help his two little girls gather their things to leave. He glanced up and smiled as I went by. He was a layman who was the person in charge of Christian education in our church. His wife, Doris, had died about a month prior to this, and he had been left alone with the two little girls, four and six and a half. I thought to myself, What a beautiful smile he has! I remembered that even at the funeral home when he had been so full of grief himself, he greeted everyone with such a wonderful smile. My heart went out to him as I saw him. What a responsibility he had now all by himself. At least I had had no children to bring up alone.

When the train pulled into Eugene, Oreg., I was thrilled and a little scared. I'd had a wonderful trip across the Northwest. Along the way I had lots of time to think and had set several goals for myself for the summer as I traveled across the country. I had made arrangements to be in a room alone so that I would have the space to work through some issues I knew I needed to settle.

Primarily, I knew I needed to close the chapter on my life with Dave. Though I had taken his ring from my left hand and put it on my right, I had not taken it off completely. I was still clinging to that time in my life. It was now almost four years since his death. During the last three years I had dated some fine young men, but I had not been able to step into a new relationship.

The first date I had was a year after Dave died. It had been so hard. My date was a friend that I had known and who had known Dave. He was fun and I enjoyed being with him, but this was a date. As strange as it may seem, I felt like an adulteress. I could hardly wait to get home, and I felt sorry for my date, for it didn't have anything to do with him as a person. In my heart I was committed to Dave. I hadn't fallen in love easily, and I did not put it aside easily.

But knowing it was healthy for me to get on with my life, and because I was lonely, I continued to date. But the moment it seemed as though any relationship could deepen, I pulled back. I was not ready.

The fact that I had been married before proved to be a difficulty to some I dated. It seemed it would be easier if I had been unhappily married. But because I had been happy, it was too threatening. Sometimes they seemed to feel in competition with Dave's memory. Perhaps I unknowingly enabled this because I had not closed this chapter in my life.

My time at the University of Oregon was one of the richest experiences of my life. It was a wonderful place to begin to live again. I did not know anyone on campus when I arrived, and so I had to make friends. No one knew me or anything about me, and so I could not depend on previous experiences to smooth my way. I had to be the one to reach out.

Before long I had a lovely circle of three or four girls with whom I developed friendships. I had opportunities to share my faith in Christ with people who did not know Him. Strangely enough, it was as I was reaching out to others that I began to be able to experience deeper healing and wholeness in my own life.

One girl who was working on a graduate degree in psychology had been told my story and came late one evening to my room to hear firsthand about what had happened in my life. She had never heard of a personal relationship with God, and she was intrigued.

One of the things that interested her about my story was the fact that after the impact of the accident, when we were waiting for the ambulance to come, Dave had talked to me quite awhile, but I could not remember the conversation. She said that she was nearing the end of her graduate degree and that she had learned how to hypnotize people. She wanted to hypnotize me so that I would be able to know what had happened during that conversation with Dave. She said it was there in my subconscious mind and could be brought forth through hypnosis. I told her I would think about it. The principle that kept me from agreeing immediately was that I had determined never to do anything that would cause me to not be in control of my own mind. She told me I could not be made to do anything that would be against my will. But I still hesitated. I had made it a practice to take even pain medicine only as long as I absolutely could not tolerate the pain.

This conviction came from an interesting source in my life. When I was about 14 years old, my family passed a bar on the way to church one Sunday morning. To our embarrassment, we saw a woman squatting on the sidewalk urinating right there in front of the bar. Compassionately, my father did not vilify her or make fun of her. He simply said, "Carolyn, my heart goes out to that dear woman. She does not know what she is doing because she is so drunk. If she knew, she would be humiliated." Right there I made up my mind that I would never drink or take anything that would cause me not to be in control of my mind and actions. As a result, now I was not willing to hand over my consciousness to someone else. I prayed about it that night and did not feel good about allowing my friend to hypnotize me. I am so grateful my father handled that scene so wisely. The principle protected me many times in the years to come.

In effect, this incident helped me close that part of the chapter. I had tried so hard to remember that scene and had never been able to recall it. I realized that there must be a reason my mind protected it. The grief might be too overwhelming. I would relinquish it all to God and leave the memory there, choosing not to anguish about it anymore. I have never regretted that decision.

I came to see that I may never know the answers to some of the questions I still had about the accident. But one thing I did know: I wanted to know God more than I wanted answers. If He at some time in my life would choose to lift the veil to my understanding, that would be fine. But I would allow nothing to interfere with my relationship with Him. I had come to the conclusion that there had been certain physical laws in operation at the moment of the accident, and God does not often intervene to change those laws, or there would be chaos. I could give the rest to Him.

In the Old Testament, there is a story of the three Hebrew children who were thrown into the fiery furnace because they refused to bow down in worship to the king. In the third chapter of Daniel the king asks Shadrach, Meshach, and Abednego if they think their God will rescue them from the fiery furnace. And the young men answered in verses 16-18: "O Nebuchadnezzar, we have no need to answer you in this matter. If that is the case, *our God whom we serve is able to deliver us* from the burning fiery furnace, and He will deliver us from your hand, O king. *But if not,* let it be known to you, O king, that we do not serve your gods, nor will we worship the gold image which you have set up" (NKJV, italics added).

These men were utterly confident that God knew where they were and in His love would bring them through whatever the circumstances by His mighty power. They chose to serve Him whether or not they were delivered from the fiery furnace! Their God would be with them. Nothing could happen to them except through His permissive hand.

I knew God had been with me in the moments of painful grief, in the times of temptation, and in the seasons of quiet joy as I was learning to communicate honestly on a deeper level with Him.

For instance, in the beginning I had known how vulnerable I was to sexual temptation because, having been married and fulfilled sexually, my body had been awakened. I now had to learn how to deal with celibacy.

First of all, I asked the Lord to protect me from any man whose attentions would prove to be a deterrent to my desires to be pure. I asked Him to put a hedge of protection around me.

Second, I asked Him to show me the mental and spiritual strategies I could use to counteract temptation when it came with pernicious intensity. I knew I needed to be prepared ahead of time.

Finally, I asked Him to show me how to channel this natural desire into creative and redemptive mission.

With a sense of awe I became aware of how God works. He would alert me with a sense of caution whenever I was drawn to someone who could have been a detriment to my Christian walk. One particular time at the University of Oregon there was an extremely articulate, handsome guy that seemed to epitomize all a girl could want. I liked him as a person and sensed his interest in me. But God cautioned me with a sense of unease. He helped me see that I could not even carry on a mild flirtation with him. I could not trifle with temptation because his values and life-style were different from mine. I knew this because I heard the other girls talking about him. It was amazing to me how specifically the Spirit directed me. I was to flee from him. That meant that I should not try to be where he was sure to be, not exchange meaningful eye contact, nor look for ways to impress him. I was not to engage in even mental fantasies about him. I was to yield my thoughts to the Lord and allow Him to give the power to control them. Because this young man had made me aware that he had noticed me and had begun to come around to where I was, I needed to have other things to consume my time so that I would not be tempted.

I had found a church near the campus. I did not have a car, and so I called the church and asked about available transportation. They said they had a church family who lived near the campus and who would be glad to pick me up each Sunday. Because of their kindness, I began to regularly attend church.

The family of a friend of mine from college attended there, and his parents invited me to share the weekend activities with them many times. The Cunninghams were wonderful to me, providing a family experience for me. This was God's way of providing an escape for me.

As I studied God's Word, I learned that Jesus used His knowledge of Scripture to combat Satan's tactics. Using 3" x 5" cards, I wrote out scriptures to carry with me so that I could memorize them. I used those scriptures aggressively, quoting them with the authority given to me as a believer in Jesus' name.

I made time at the beginning of each day as faithfully as I could to spend time in prayer. When I was in the throes of spiritual battle sometimes, I found I could not pray for any length of time then, because it only caused me to focus in on the area of temptation more. I had to be able to give a quick cry for help and power to the Lord, knowing I was already up-to-date in prayer for this matter.

One strategy I learned was that when thoughts of temptation would suddenly assail me, I would send up a quick prayer to God for His help and power and then would instantly switch my mind to some healthy fantasy. For instance, if I were driving down the street and suddenly temptation would overwhelm me, I would pray a short prayer and then immediately switch my thoughts to the fantasy that I could buy any house on that street I wanted. I would begin to look at the houses and pretend that money was no object and decide which one of the houses I would buy and how I would decorate it. My thoughts would become so wrapped up in my imagination that the battle was won. I had not tried to fight Satan mentally; I had allowed God to take over the battle as I moved on mentally. It was astounding how effective this was to help bring my thoughts into captivity. I planned ahead on possible wholesome fantasies that I could count on intriguing my interest at the time I needed them!

Sometimes, I would have to bind the power of Satan by verbally speaking aloud in order to emphatically resist him. I would say, "In the name of Jesus Christ of Nazareth, and by the authority of His shed blood and His Word, I command you to depart from me right now. I resist you in His power and in His might. You will have no more power to bind me up because of Jesus. Amen." No matter what my feelings were, my will was set to allow the power of God to work.

I determined not to feed the wrongful expression of what God planned as beautiful natural desire. There were times I would have to get up and leave a room if a scene on television would become too romantic, simply because it would start my train of thought in a way I was too vulnerable to control at that time. It was my way to cooperate with God in obedience.

I stayed in Oregon three months, when I packed to come home. I looked back at the small, one-windowed room with its narrow bed and single desk just before I closed the door. This room had been a sanctuary. But now all was packed. I was ready to leave. I was truly closing a door, literally and symbolically. I had closed the chapter of my life with Dave. I had taken off my wedding ring. I had put all my mementos away in a box—a precious keepsake. I was ready to live again.

David and
Carolyn Miller,
wedding day,
December 18, 1954.

David Miller, first-year
seminary student, 1955.

Carolyn Miller, Junior at Olivet
Nazarene University, 1957.

Oregon, Mo., Church of the Nazarene, David Miller's first pastorate.

The car in which David and Carolyn were riding at the time of the accident, 1955.

Car and station wagon after the accident

After the accident

After the accident (front view)

Lyle and Margaret Eckley with daughters Carolyn, Jeanne, and Kathleen, 1955.

Vernon and Carolyn Lunn, wedding day, April 9, 1960.

Susan, Vernon, and Sharon Lunn in 1959, shortly after Doris' death.

*"O my soul, why be so gloomy
and discouraged? Trust in God!
I shall again praise him
for His wondrous help;
he will make me smile again,
for he is my God!"*

PS. 43:5, TLB

A Bride in Beige Silk

Oh, magnify the Lord with me, and let us
exalt His name together.   PS. 34:3, NKJV

One of Summit Expedition's exceptional instructors,
Rick Vander Kam, was asked, "Hey, Rick, what are you
going to be doing five years from now?"

His answer is worth remembering. He began, "I don't
know."

To which his friend remarked, "What's the matter?
Don't you have dreams? Don't you have goals? Don't you
have plans?"

Rick answered, "Of course I do. I've written down my
goals and I've got incredible, specific plans, but I happen
to be following Somebody who is *notoriously unpredictable.*"[1]

In beginning this new chapter of my life I, too, had
specific plans! Then I discovered just how full of surprises
God's ways could be. It began almost as soon as I arrived
home from Oregon. I was excited because I had a new
school where I would teach a second- and third-grade
combination. I was challenged with the *now* of my life, but
I was making plans for the future.

An opportunity came to make application to teach

abroad at one of the U.S. Army bases in a foreign country. I had always wanted to travel, and this sounded wonderful. I went to downtown Kansas City to the government building and started the procedure for application.

As I looked at the countries where bases were located, I grew excited when I saw some European countries where our church was opening new mission work. It would be a thrill to be a part of a different culture, perhaps learn a language, and help win people to Christ in a newly begun church. What a tremendous opportunity for me as a single person who had no obligations. I decided to follow the necessary procedures, to open the way for what might be an option for my life in the future.

Second, I began to look at the various universities near me to check out their graduate programs in guidance and counseling. In this way I could teach full-time and go to school at night and in the summers. I also entertained the thought of going someplace I had never been before, as I had gone to Oregon, and taking a year off to pursue my studies full-time. This last sounded like an adventure—getting my education but enjoying the process!

I was trying to find God's will for this new chapter of my life and pursuing all the possible options so that I could best find His plan. In the midst of all this adventurous planning I was enjoying living with four other girls in a house across the street from the church we attended.

One Friday afternoon early in September, I came home from school and parked my car across the street in the church parking lot. I often did this, as our street was such a busy street you could not park there. Gathering my books and things together, I got out of the car. As I turned to close the door, I was startled to find that the young widower I told you about was coming out of the church a few steps away. I taught a Sunday School class in the Junior High Department, and since he was in charge of Christian education, we talked briefly about some upcoming plans.

Then, casually he said, "Carolyn, I wonder if you would like to go out to dinner with me two weeks from today?"

I was shocked! I tried not to let him know by the expression on my face, though. One likes to act as if she has been asked for a date at least once before! You see, all I could think of in that moment were the letters I had received from church friends while I was in Oregon. After a couple of months they began to write, and ask questions like: "Do you think Vernon will begin dating soon? If so, who do you think he will date?" I had smiled and wondered who it would be if he did, but never once had I considered myself a candidate!

There were three reasons for this. First of all, Vernon was 11 years older than I and ran around in a different circle of friends. Second, I had known of the Lunn family all of my life because Dr. M. Lunn (Vernon's father) and Vernon's brother Bud had consecutively been managers of our church's publishing house for many years. I deeply admired and respected Vernon. His wife's illness and death had been a real loss to our church. We had all grieved with him. But I knew him only in a working relationship at church.

Third, after Dave died, I had made the statement that there was one thing I knew I would never do. (You know about that kind of statement?) It was: "I will never marry a widower with children." I did not want someone looking at me as a young schoolteacher and thinking that I would make a wonderful mother for their children, but not love me for myself.

So when Vernon spoke to me about a date, I was not prepared. But when he smiled that beautiful smile, I decided I wanted to go. Then he said, "Carolyn, I don't want you to think that I would be ashamed to be seen with you by what I am going to say, but I have been thinking about our dating. So many people know the story of your husband and of my wife that they might be interested in knowing if we were going out with one another. Would you consider dating secretly so that we could decide ourselves how we felt about dating without the input of a lot of other people?" That made a great deal of sense to me because, you see, I knew about the letters! So I agreed.

I was nervous about my date with Vernon. I held him in such esteem, and he was a mature, classy man. There were only two couples who knew we were dating and only one of my roommates. It seemed we went to every restaurant around Kansas City we could find. But with all our caution, we would still run into people we knew! When I got home, I would have to call them and ask them if they would mind not telling anyone they had seen us, and I would tell them why. Everyone I talked to seemed to understand and entered into the secret willingly with us!

It wasn't long before I began to realize that when I had made the statement that I didn't want to marry a man with children, I had not known of Vernon Lunn. As I came to really know him, my appreciation for him as a man of deep personal integrity only grew. We shared so many things in common. Our backgrounds were similar. We had been raised on the same value system. Our personal goals were in harmony. And the more I was around him, the less the difference in our ages mattered.

Vernon did not rush me—but he seemed to know how he felt about me very soon. On our third date, when he took me to the door, he simply put his arms around me and held me quietly as he talked about what he hoped our relationship could be. I will never forget that in his arms I felt as if I had come home. I felt cherished, and for the first time I began to think differently about my relationship with him.

But I was shaken. I realized I was not dealing with a man alone. He had two precious little girls, his family, his personal friends who had loved Doris, his wife, dearly.

How would they accept me? How would my family and friends respond? How would we work through all these relationships?

As my feelings for Vernon deepened, I went to the Lord and began to pour out my heart to Him. I told Him that this wasn't exactly what I had had in mind for my life! The only stepmother I knew anything about was the one in the story of Cinderella, and she was mean and ugly and had a long nose! And though I could qualify for one of those characteristics, I did not think I was mean or ugly! I was 25 years old, but I felt too young to take on the responsibility of a 5-year-old and a 7½-year-old. I also sought counsel from my pastor and his wife.

I knew I personally would need the special hand of God on my life. If I would love these little girls as they should be loved, it would require a stretching and strengthening of my capacity to love. I could not do it on my own. I knew I was coming to love Vernon. I prayed ever more earnestly that God's love would be free to flow through me if this was His will for our lives. I asked God to cleanse my heart and life of anything that would be harmful to developing a loving, healthy relationship as a family. For a little more than four years now, I had had only my own schedule and needs to be concerned about. It would be an adjustment now to think of a family budget, of the inability to go out unless we had a baby-sitter, the responsibility of caring for a home.

Vernon and I had to learn to communicate with each other. I discovered it is difficult for Vernon to share his innermost feelings. He doesn't sit still very long for lengthy, intense conversations. He is a doer. He shows his love by doing things for his loved ones, helping them in any way he can. On the other hand, I love to learn to know someone through talking and sharing. I am comfortable expressing my love verbally, and I have a need to be affirmed verbally of love.

We knew that when two people marry, it is more than those two people coming together. You each bring all that you are to the relationship, including your parents' influence, your cultural background, and your religious training. And in our case we added the relationships with former spouses. Because we had been married before, we understood the complexities of blending our lives together. We were more aware the second time around of the commitment and love needed to make a marriage work. Vernon had been married for 10 years! I had been married for only eight months. I had more to learn!

As we learned to know one another, Vernon became my best friend, and our love grew. Both of us had the confidence that God was affirming our relationship. And in my personal prayer, God had promised me through His Word to increase my capacity for love by His power.

During the Christmas season we became engaged to be married. We did not make a formal announcement, but we no longer made an effort to keep our relationship a secret. It was fun to watch the reaction of people as they began to see us together. The surprise! The wonder that we had been able to keep it a secret for so long. Vernon's closest friends were wonderful to me, and I know it had to be a difficult adjustment for them. My friends were beautifully supportive also. And our families were tremendous.

How differently this new chapter of my life was being revealed! I had not known that God had a loving husband in mind for me. God truly is creative and unpredictable!

We planned to be married in April. Vernon owned a lovely ranch-style home in Leawood, Kans., a suburb of Kansas City. After Doris died, Vernon had rented the home to a developer and had taken the girls to live with his mother and father. He gave his renters the notice that he would not be renewing their lease, as he would be needing his home.

During the weeks between our engagement and wedding, we spent time with Vernon's girls, Sharon and Susan. We tried very hard to include them in our love and planning. We needed to help them feel secure in this, another change in their lives. They were so willing to accept me. What an answer to prayer!

Early one Sunday morning, three weeks before we were to be married, Vernon called to tell me that his home was on fire. The neighbors had called his parents' home to notify him that the house was burning. He called me as he was leaving to go out to Leawood.

The night before, the renters had a late party. They had been drinking and carelessly smoking in the living room. Ashes had fallen on the couch and smoldered for a time before bursting into flames. The living room was on the opposite side of the house from the bedrooms, and the fire spread to the grand piano next to the couch; soon the whole end of the house was in flames and spreading rapidly. The renters had been sleeping and were overcome by smoke. They were rescued by the firemen. The house was gone.

As we walked through the remains later, the acrid smell of smoke blanketed the air as we gazed at the devastation. Vernon had rented the home completely furnished, so everything was gone. I felt such pain for Vernon and the girls. The girls had lost not only their mother but now their home as well. In some of the rooms, the heat from the fire had been so intense that only ashes and melted globs of plastic from phones, etc., remained.

The scripture "Set your affection on things above, not on things on the earth" (Col. 3:2, KJV) came to mind. Now I truly knew that material things could not be a top priority of your life. They could be gone in a moment of time. As we drove home that day, I asked the Lord to help me make eternal values the center of my life—that from that moment of time, I would learn to keep material possessions in their proper perspective.

111

Once again God began to bring good out of what seemed to be a catastrophe. I hadn't anticipated any difficulties in moving into the home in which Vernon had lived with Doris. I thought it was decorated beautifully. But I think that sometimes God looks at us and says, "Now that's one problem she doesn't need to have," and so He allows events to take place that in the end He can bring about to our good. He did not cause those men to drink and become careless smoking. But He did not interfere with the physical laws set in motion by such carelessness. I was spared living in circumstances that might have been a problem in some low moment in the days ahead, and we all as a family were able to begin a new life together in an environment we had created and built ourselves.

And so our plans were changed. I guess one of the most permanent things in life is change! We decided to rebuild the house on the old foundation. I was living in a one-bedroom apartment now; and we decided that after we were married, Vernon and I would live in the apartment, and the girls would live with their grandparents until school was out, when we could get into our home.

It is significant that all of us, at some point in our lives, have what seem to be insurmountable problems arise. But we discover His healing plan for each one of us is exactly right for our needs. He teaches us how to perceive the now, how to risk living with an unshakable faith in the midst of pain and difficulties, which are a part of every life. He teaches us how to be fully alive to Him in those moments. As B. Howland says:

> For a long time
> > it had seemed to me that life was about to
> > > begin—real life.
> But there was always some obstacle in the way.
> Something to be got through first,
> > some unfinished business;
> > time to be served,

a debt to be paid.
Then life would begin.
At last it dawned on me that those obstacles
were my life.[2]

The night before our wedding I was alone in my apartment, thinking about my coming marriage. For a moment, the awesome responsibility I was assuming the next day overwhelmed me. And then God reminded me again of the promise He had given to me that He would stretch my capacity to love—that He would make adequate where I was inadequate—and I was at peace again.

As I joyfully anticipated my marriage and the intimacies I would know, I marveled at how at peace I was. As I pondered this with gratitude, my mind flashed back to a time almost six years before.

It was Thanksgiving time, and I had joined my family in Milwaukee from college to attend the wedding of a family friend. I was feeling low because Dave and I had been having problems in our dating relationship. I knew that I loved him, but I was afraid of getting hurt. He had dated quite a bit more than I, and I was afraid to trust him. This wedding scene was causing me to do some serious thinking.

The young bride had been married before, but her husband had died. As the ceremony progressed, you could see the deep love this young couple had for one another. And when they kissed at the end of the ceremony, you could sense the strong physical attraction between them. I sat there nonplussed. How could she love this second man so much and be willing to enter the sexual intimacies of marriage with another man when I knew she had loved her first husband deeply? Torn apart by my feelings of love for Dave, I just could not understand, as I could not fathom myself being able to do that.

As I watched them, I thought deeply about it. The only reasoning I could accept in my mind was that each man filled his very particular place in her life. Neither one could take the place of the other. Each was unique. Though they might have some characteristics in common, each man would bring something different and special into her life. They would not be competing with each other, for there was no way to compare them. Therefore she could respond with deep commitment and passion, knowing she was being true to herself and to them. Each had their own chapter in her life.

As I sat there in my apartment that night, I realized that the reason I had such peace was that six years ago, before I had even married my first husband, God had used that setting to prepare me for this moment in my life! I could remember the time of my wedding with Dave and be grateful I had known and loved him, but the deep grief and pain were gone. As I realized how deeply God cares about preparing us for life, I felt loved.

These were two wonderful men that God had brought into my life. So different and yet each shared some common threads. Both had a growing personal relationship with Jesus Christ. Both had a strong work ethic and inner drive. No one had to push them to get them to move. They were already on the way. Both had a deep compassion for others.

Our wedding was very small. It was held in the prayer chapel at the seminary with only our families there and our pastor and wife. My sister Jeanne and Vernon's brother Bud stood up with us. My father assisted in the marriage ceremony. I wore a simple two-piece beige silk dress with a little hat and veil. Vernon wore a dark suit. It was a beautiful, sacred, covenant-making ceremony. On my ring, Vernon had engraved the Scripture reference for the verse we were claiming for our life together.

"Oh, magnify the Lord with me,
and let us exalt His name together" (Ps. 34:3, NKJV).

*"You turned my wailing
into dancing;
you removed my sackcloth
and clothed me with joy."*

PS. 30:11

■ııı 8

More than a Theory

If God speaks to me anywhere, I think
it is in our daily lives. I wonder
how much of God's grace I experience . . .
and how much I'm capable of experiencing.[1]

TIM HANSEL

Jill Briscoe has said: "One of the greatest miracles in my life has taken place as God has taken four incompatible people and one incompatible dog and said, 'Now make a family!'" I couldn't agree with her more!

When the minister said a few words over our bowed heads in our marriage ceremony, I became not only a bride but also a mother. I discovered early that it is one thing to be a teacher and think you know how children should be raised, and quite another to be the mother. It had been my decision to give up my teaching and become a full-time mother and homemaker. I felt that it would take all my time and energy to do my part to help us become a family. And it did! With all the trauma we had had in our lives, we needed to learn how to relate to one another.

Vernon and I had only those first couple of months while our home was being rebuilt to be alone. In that time, I was completing the school year as a teacher and trying to decorate a home. I did not have the full care of the girls yet. We had a chance to enjoy one another in those first weeks without the total responsibility of anyone else.

A fire contractor was needed to build our home because of their expertise in knowing how to rebuild after a fire. They knew what had to be replaced and what could be salvaged. Because the fire had been fought with foam rather than water, we were happy to discover that our furnace could be cleaned and reused. But we learned that even though flames had not destroyed things totally, smoke damage had been so severe that everything else would need to be replaced.

I knew nothing about decorating a home. My family had always lived in a home owned by the church; and because Mother's health was poor, we usually made only minor changes, such as paint colors in the rooms. I knew nothing about window treatments, wallpaper, furniture styles, etc.

With intrepid heart I began. The wife of the man who had originally built the house had helped her husband decorate his model homes. She was our friend, so I asked for her help. As we looked at wallpaper books, fabric swatches, paint chips, carpet samples, and window treatment sketches, we had great fun choosing what we needed. When we finished, Vernon and I had a new beginning together.

We moved into our new home in July. Now came the real adjustments: for Sharon and Susan, a new mother and a home without all the familiar furniture and mementos; and for Vernon and me, adapting to each other and to our mutual role as parents. My life truly was a performance for which there was no rehearsal!

In thinking of my relationship with the girls, I knew I had to earn their love and respect. They must have time to learn to know me and feel safe with me. I had to learn to know and genuinely love them for themselves and not just because they belonged to Vernon. I asked myself, "How would you treat the girls if right now you had all the feelings of love for them that you want to have? What are some of the things you would do for them?" I took a piece of paper and began to write down my thoughts.

1. I would spend some special time each day with them individually, trying to learn their personalities, the things they like to do.

2. I would try to be creative in making healing prayer a part of the process of our learning to love each other.

3. I would look for ways to just have fun together.

4. I would make sure they looked as clean and pretty as I could possibly help them look.

5. I would make sure they felt a part of the love relationship Vernon and I enjoyed. They must never feel left out.

6. I would be willing to admit it when I made a mistake. I would not gain their trust if I was unwilling to be vulnerable.

7. I would help them feel unthreatened about talking about their mother and their life together as a family. This would mean being so spiritually attuned to the Lord that I would be able to handle any threatening feeling *I* might have. How I would need His help!

8. I would be careful and sensitive to our situation as I disciplined.

9. I would try to be the best example of Christian womanhood and femininity before them that I could possibly be, because I would care about the women they would someday become.

10. I would love their dad. If they were sure of my love for him, this would give them a sense of security.

I liked the girls very much and wanted to love them with the depth of feeling I would have if I had given them birth. I prayed for God to give me that kind of love. I decided to *act as if* I possessed those feelings. I would do the things that I had listed, trusting God to stretch my capacity to love until those feelings would be mine, in His way and timing.

A second marriage in which you are blending a family can be very difficult. I know that the fact that Vernon is the gentle, strong man that he is, and Sharon and Susan are the loving, open persons they are, made it easier for me to be what I needed to be. It would have been so hard for me if it hadn't been for their desire to be open to me.

In order to spend some time with each girl during the day, God gave me the idea to have a "hug time." I would find some place where we could be alone, either at home, on a walk, or taking a ride in the car. I would put an arm around her, and I would focus entirely on her, gradually helping her feel at ease with me so that she could share.

I learned that Sharon was a typical firstborn child who was a caretaker. This feeling had been underscored during the time of her mother's death, when people had come up to Sharon and said, "You will have to help take care of your little sister now, Sharon, and help your daddy." She was a deeply compassionate person, who even then knew she wanted to be a nurse. It wasn't easy for her to share her innermost feelings, but gradually she began to feel secure enough to express herself. She loved to stay inside the house and play there. She was not at all athletic. She had a strong will but was not abrasive. She would not talk back to me, but there were times when you knew she might be sitting down on the outside, but she was standing up on the inside! Sharon was able to stand alone if she had to. She wanted to have peer approval, but she was not controlled by it. I don't remember ever spanking her. She could entertain herself, but she enjoyed playing with Susie.

With Susie, you always knew how she felt about things. She was articulate and had a tremendous imagination. She could spend hours pretending she was playing house, etc. She could be very independent. She spoke to others when she wanted to, and at other times she would go on her way, blithely ignoring all. She could be hilarious, making us all laugh with her witty one-liners. Sharon was her best audience! Because she was only three when her mother became seriously ill and only four when she died, she had a lot of fears. Susan had more of a battle about needing peer approval.

Then there was Vernon. He is probably the world's most organized man! He would carry a yellow legal pad around on which he had organized his day. When we were first married, he thought I needed help, and so he bought a blackboard on which he wrote down the things he felt I should get done that day! When I would not do them, or at least not do them in the order in which he thought they should be done, he would get frustrated! Finally, I said to him one day, "Honey, if it helps you psychologically to write those things down, you go right ahead and do it; but if you don't mind, I will do them in the order in which I feel they need to be done." He is a morning person. Early morning is the best time of day for him. I am a night person. I can stay up till all hours, reading, sewing, writing, or whatever. I'll never forget the morning he came and stood by the side of the bed, looking down at me, and said, "Honey, *you* have so much to do today!" I said, "Vernon, please don't come to me before I even get my head up off the pillow and tell me how much I've got to do! It's all right for you to talk about how much you have to do today, but it's too early to talk about me!"

God knew how much we needed each other to have better balance in our lives! How glad we were that in trying to learn to accept each other, God gave all four of us a good sense of humor to help us in our "adjusting"!

We learned the value of healing prayer. Susan was a philosophical child. She never just accepted things. She had to reason them through. As I mentioned, she had a lot of fears. As she learned to depend on me, she began to be afraid to be away from me for fear that I would be gone when she came back. She had a hard time going to sleep at night. Sharon and Susan slept in twin beds in the same room, and often at night we would hear Susan say to Sharon, "Please sing to me, Sharon. I can't sleep." Then you would hear Sharon sweetly singing some little song to her. Gradually, she would go to sleep.

But there were some nights when she would come and wake me around 2:30 in the morning. She would tap me on the forehead and say, "Mommy, I can't sleep." And I would say, "Susie, that now makes two of us!" But I would slip out of bed so as not to wake Vernon, and we would go into the living room and talk for a while. She would share her fears with me.

She also had trouble with her concept of God. In those early morning hours, I began to realize how God had prepared me for just these moments, back when I was 22 years old in college and going through my own questioning period. He had helped me search out my own beliefs, so that in these moments I could speak with clarity about Him and how much He loved and cared for this precious little girl. How thankful I was for His foresight in helping me be ready. Susan and I built a bridge of love in those early morning hours that stretched across the years to a time when she would need me when she went through a period of doubt in college. She allowed me to talk to her then, I believe, because of the value of those moments many years earlier.

Another time, Susan was invited to spend the night with a little girlfriend of hers. She didn't want to leave me, and she was afraid she wouldn't sleep at night. My heart grieved so for Susan, and I wanted her to be able to be freed from this deep fear. I called her into her bedroom so that we could talk alone and told her what a wonderful time she would have if she would go. She finally agreed she would go. Then we got down on our knees beside the bed and prayed that God would heal her of her fears and help her be at peace while she was at her friend's so that she could sleep. I promised her when she left that I would call her friend's mother about what time they would probably go to bed, and then I would pray for her at that exact time. She could trust me to do that.

All that evening, I have to confess, I expected the phone to ring, and Susan would be wanting us to come and get her. But she did not. And when it came to the time that I knew they would be going to bed, I slipped off by myself and began to pray for Susan. I was in the center bedroom where it was like a little sitting room with a couch. I knelt down to pray. As I prayed, such a burden came over me for Susan that I found myself praying with my head buried in the carpet. I felt this was such a pivotal time in her life. I prayed not only that she would be healed of her fears but also that she would understand the power of prayer. I continued praying until I knew I had prayed through. I had the assurance that God had heard my prayer and that He was going to heal Susan.

We never heard from her all night! The next day, I have to admit, I was anxious to hear how she had done. So I called the girl's mother and asked her not to tell Susan I had called. Mary said that Susan had told her when it was time to go to bed, "My mommy is praying that I will go to sleep, so I have to hurry and get in bed." She said that she zipped up her sleeping bag and listened quietly to the other little girls talking for a while, but soon went sound asleep and slept till morning! What an answer to prayer.

When she came home, we talked about how God answered prayer, and we took the time right then to bow our heads and thank Jesus for what He had done. And God

123

began to heal Susan from that day on, just as He had promised me.

The girls and I had great fun together. As a mother who loved to imagine, I often had a party with them for no reason at all. The neighbor kids were frequently at our house. But some of the best fun was getting ready for Dad to come home each day. I tried to make it fun and make him feel special too. Oh, I don't mean to say that every day was a party, because there *were* days when my day had gone all wrong, and I would feel I needed to turn up the corner of my apron or something, just to let Vernon know when he walked in the door that I was fragile because I had had a hard day. But my goal was to have a positive attitude. Fair or not, I believe the mother often sets the atmosphere of the home. And because I tried, I succeeded more often than not.

I love to sew, and I would try to make the girls pretty dresses so that they would feel pretty. One Christmas I worked especially hard at making them some red velveteen dresses. They looked nice when they walked out the door that Christmas Sunday, and I felt proud.

When we arrived at church, the girls ran in ahead of us. Quickly taking off their coats, they hurried along to their Sunday School classrooms. I heard people exclaiming to them as they hurried down the hall, "Susan and Sharon, what beautiful dresses you have on! Did Carolyn make them for you?" And of course they said that I had. You see, I had felt as though the people at church were watching to see how I would do as a mother for Sharon and Susie. In fact, I had been afraid to correct them in church for fear they would say, "Look how she is treating them. If she does that at church, what does she do at home?"

In that moment, as I heard people complimenting the girls and was so proud, the Lord came and spoke in my heart. He said, "Carolyn, do you see the way you are feeling? You are making those dresses for the sake of how people will perceive you. Won't you let Me help you forget what people say and have your motivation be that you make those dresses just because you love the girls?" I wanted that so badly in that moment that I slipped into the ladies' rest room and entered one of the stalls and stood there praying brokenly, asking the Lord to help me get beyond what people said or did, and learn to do what I did just for love and no other reason. God showed me I wasn't the only one who had ever done what I was doing as a stepmother, and I was not the last, so I needn't have so much pride in my heart. God was faithful and removed the wrong motivation and helped me to want to sew for beauty that could come to the girls and for no other reason!

I hate to admit it, but I had a lot of growing up to do in order to be the person I needed to be. At first, I can remember feeling a little lonely, because of the close relationship between Vernon and the girls. He had had their total care for a couple of years, and they depended on him. The bond of love they shared was beautiful. But sometimes I felt on the outside. If I was not careful, because of my own immaturity, I would indulge in a little pity party. I was too ashamed to admit my hurt to Vernon or anyone else, and so I was glad that I could go to the Lord. I knew He knew me better than anyone else and loved me anyway! But I also knew that He wanted to help me do better. I asked for His help, and He gave it to me. I would join in their conversations about their life before as a family. I refused to allow myself to sit in a corner feeling threatened and pouting. I learned to laugh with them and to genuinely enjoy their delight in one another; and soon, because God stretched me, I felt a part too!

There were many times that I would have to ask the girls to forgive me when I handled a situation wrong. It seemed this would often happen when I would tuck them in at night and pray with them before they went to sleep. We would talk about the day, and I would try to express my feelings to them. I would tell them how inadequate I often felt. How sometimes my reactions would be a result of frustration. I would ask their forgiveness. How important that time was!

Some of my frustrations would come at the time of discipline. One day Sharon and Susan were doing some kind of a craft. Sharon used my sewing scissors, which I felt should only be used on material and not on paper, to cut out her paper project. When I took them away from her and corrected her, she said, "Well, my mother always let me do it!"

In that moment, the most awful feeling of resentment and frustration welled up in me. I thought to myself, Oh, she did, did she! Well, that's just too bad. But I didn't say it out loud. I had learned that when I sense something like that happening within me, I better deal with it right away. I excused myself and asked the girls to answer the phone if they needed to; I was going to my room for a while. I sat in the quietness of the room and asked the Lord to show me what it was that was eating away at my inner emotions. We shouldn't ask if we don't really want to know. For sometimes the Lord shows us ourselves, and we would like to think we are a much nobler person than is revealed! And that is what happened this day.

As God spoke to my heart, He showed me that I had a deep resentment in my heart against Vernon's first wife, Doris, and his mother. You see, intellectually, I understood that the last two years of Doris's life, she had been very ill. And I knew that she had allowed the girls to get away with more than she would have if she had been well. It takes a lot of energy to discipline children, and sometimes it is a lot easier to say, "Oh, go ahead," when we should have hung in there and said, "No." On top of that they had lived a year with Grandmother, who thought her little granddaughters could do no wrong. And now, along comes the stepmother, who is not physically ill, who is not a grandmother, and who needs to discipline; and I resented being placed in the position of being the big, bad ogre!

Intellectually, I understood it all; emotionally, I was struggling. I was not proud of the deep resentment the Lord showed me I had. But God did not show it to me to rub my nose in it. He showed it to me so that I would be aware it was there and to ask Him to remove it from me and help me be the person I needed to be in this situation. A much bigger person than that! I prayed and asked the Lord to remove the resentment from my heart. I knew only He could do that. I asked Him to give me the faith to believe that because I had asked, He would do it, no matter what my feelings may be. I willed to give it all to Him. I left the bedroom with a sense of peace that God would work His wonderful power in my heart. And He did take the resentment away.

Through it all, my love for Vernon and Sharon and Susan grew. Somehow, by God's help, I knew we were going to be able to be a real family!

"Weeping may endure for a night,
but joy comes in the morning."

PS. 30:5, NKJV

From Grief to Joy

The rubber of faith meets the road of
reality under hardship . . . the trueness of
one's belief is revealed in pain.
Genuineness and character
are unveiled in misfortune.
Faith is at its best, not in three-piece suits
on Sunday mornings or at VBS
on summer days, but at hospital bedsides,
cancer wards, and cemeteries.[1]   MAX LUCADO

I tried to keep a large brown pottery cookie jar full of cookies, ready for after-school snacks. The jar sat on the brick hearth of the fireplace in our country kitchen. One afternoon, Sharon and her friend from school were raiding the cookie jar as I was beginning preparation for the evening meal.

While I cooked, they regaled me with lively conversation about their day. As we laughed and talked, I noticed that Sharon's friend was really looking me over. Every time Sharon would say something to me, she would swivel her head to see how I would respond. When I would say something to Sharon, she would immediately turn to see Sharon's response. Her transparent curiosity intrigued me!

When she left, I said to Sharon, "Do I look strange today?"

"No, Mom. Why?" I told her how I had noticed her friend staring at me and then watching us closely as we responded to one another. She laughed and said offhandedly, "Well, Mom, on the way home from school today, I told her our story. You know, about how my mother died and your husband died. She wanted to come and see you, because she had never been around a stepmother before!"

This was a reminder to me that I was not the only one making adjustments! The girls were well aware of the differences in their life now. We had been married about a year and a half by then, and I reflected on our process of adjustment to one another. Only a couple of months after we were married, the girls had felt comfortable calling me Mother. I had not forced the issue. We had talked about the options, and then I had left it up to them. I had been so thankful the girls were able to do this.

It *was* an adventure, learning to be a bride and a mother all at once. I liked being a homemaker, but with the added responsibilities of motherhood, I had not realized how much *work* it all is. I can remember falling into bed one night, utterly exhausted, and Vernon quietly saying to me, "Honey, I'm going to leave more of the care of the girls to you now." I was startled! You've got to be kidding! I thought. I was already taking care of them, wasn't I? But as the days unfolded, I came to understand that Vernon helped me with their care considerably more than most other men helped their wives.

Soon the time had come when I wanted to give birth to a child. All of us were so excited when we found out that I was pregnant. It wasn't long before we found out I was *very* pregnant! The doctor was fairly certain that I was going to have a multiple birth! About three months later, he suggested I have a test to determine how many babies I was carrying. When he told me the results, I could hardly wait to tell Vernon. When he heard, he didn't know whether to go to the finance company or the architect first! We were definitely going to have twins, but the doctor thought there might be another baby there also. Would we have triplets?

It hardly seemed real at first. We talked about names, and how small the room was that we had planned for *one* baby—trying to comprehend what a difference it would make in our life-style to have two, and maybe three, babies at once!

But one morning when I was nearing my sixth month of pregnancy, I lay in my bed with anxiety coursing through me. I knew something was wrong. I began to have labor pains, and I was heartsick. Vernon had already gone to work, so I called out for Sharon and Susan. My sister Kathleen was there to help me, but she slept too soundly to hear me. The girls came right away and then called Kathleen. We called the doctor, and he told me to come to the hospital immediately. We called Vernon. I did not cry. I was just trying to deal with the basic necessity of getting ready to go to the hospital.

I will never forget the scene that morning when Vernon arrived and we left to go to the hospital. One little girl sat on the sofa, and another stood behind the big overstuffed chair, crying as if their hearts would break. Here were two children who were facing more trauma and death than many of us do in our adult lives. My heart ached for them.

The doctor asked us to go to a different hospital than we had planned. He wanted us to go to St. Mary's Hospital in Kansas City, which he felt was better equipped to handle this kind of emergency. When we pulled into the emergency entrance of the hospital, Dad Lunn and Vernon's brother Bud were there to meet us!

In those days, the husbands were not involved in the birthing process, so I was whisked away to the labor room by myself. I was frightened of the unknown, but I still kept hoping that my babies could be saved.

As I lay on the labor table, my stomach seemed a huge mound protecting my babies. The nurses kept checking for the babies' heartbeat. They told me they wanted to give me only the minimum pain reliever so that the babies could help fight the battle to live. The tears slipped down the sides of my face onto the pillow. I was really fearful now. The babies would be so small. Would they be able to survive?

As the labor pains grew closer together and more intense, they wheeled me into the delivery room. In the trauma and pain of the moment I had to depend on the prayers of my family and friends.

The babies did not live. They were red-haired identical twin girls. The third baby was not completely formed. After the birth, I heard someone ask, "Is the mother Catholic or Protestant?" I knew they were asking in order to give the last rites if we were Catholic. It was a Catholic hospital. The reality of their death hit me with thundering force. It was difficult when they wheeled me to my room. It was close to the nursery, and I could hear the newborn babies crying. Vernon was waiting in the room for me. He held me. We hurt so badly there seemed to be few words we could say as we reached out to each other.

The doctor gave me a medical explanation for the babies' deaths, but I don't remember it. I do recall that he said that it was one in so many million cases that this happened, and that the babies would have had difficulties surviving had they lived. He encouraged me, saying, "Carolyn, you make beautiful babies! The twins were beautifully formed. Don't be afraid to try again. But I would suggest you wait about a year."

As we dealt with our loss, I realized that each one of us handles his grief in the best way he can. I found that Vernon tended to withdraw within himself to work it through. He couldn't talk about it much, though he felt the loss as deeply as I did. As is his way, he expressed his love through action—cooking, doing laundry, caring for the girls. He made me feel cherished by the way he helped with the simplest tasks. His dry sense of humor helped us all to laugh again.

During this time I realized that it would be impossible for Vernon to know how to meet all my emotional needs. In fact, it would be wrong to expect him to do so. To bind him up with my expectations would only increase his trauma and mine, as no one person can meet all of another's needs. But I would need to keep my heart open to him.

I am more verbal, so I needed to talk to my family and friends, and this helped immensely. However, they could only do so much. I basked in their love, but I had to work through my grief alone.

There is an aloneness about life. I am not talking about loneliness here. I am talking about the solitary time when each of us in our innermost being must come to grips with our package of life. Alone, we decide on the attitudes and responses we will choose. Alone, we think through the issues, the feelings, the consequences, the realities facing us, and the results of that thinking form our character.

Gail Sheehy, in her book *Character,* wrote:

> The root of the word "character" is the Greek word for engraving. It refers to the enduring marks left by life that set one apart as an individual.
>
> Distinctive marks of character are carved by parental and religious imprinting, by a child's early interactions with siblings, peers and significant others. The manners of one's social class, the soil in which one grows up remain indelible. It is also marked by where a person stood at great divides in his or her nation's history.
>
> But what matters even more, is how many of

the passages of adult life have been met and mastered, and what he or she has done with the life accidents dealt by fate.[2]

I sought once again to see how Christ responded in His adult life to the realities He faced. In His moments of acute decision He understood the need for solitary reflection. I saw how this helped Him focus on His Father. Alone, yet in His Father's presence, He triumphantly met life's challenges.

In my aloneness, I was aware of my Heavenly Father's presence and of the hunger in my heart just to be with Him. There was an excruciating awareness that once again I was at the absolute end of my own abilities and resources to deal with my grief. Daily, I had to continue to learn to fling myself in absolute abandon on God. It is not easy, because it is not natural. Only the mighty power of God can transform us by His Holy Spirit until it becomes supernaturally natural to respond in this way. To come to Him first with all the happenings of our lives, our blessings as well as our needs. To make Him our closest friend.

Now that I've tried both ways, I know there is no substitute for the life lived in dependence on God. It brings a joy and serenity that can be produced in no other way.

After the death of the babies, the silence in the house shattered me most. There were no cries of a newborn baby. No lullabies wafting their soft melody in the air. I would try to fill the silence with music or turn on the TV, but nothing could assuage its emptiness. I would walk into the room we had planned to use as the nursery. We had not started to redecorate it yet, and so it looked like what it was—a small sitting room. There was no evidence we had ever expected a baby. I would stand there and sob, my tears splashing on the carpet, and think about the little girls I would never know until I saw them in heaven someday.

I couldn't pray. My mind seemed numbed. I paced the floor with my arms hugging my body as grief tore through me. Finally, when I was totally exhausted emotionally, I fell across the small couch. I cried out, "O Jesus, please help me." That was all. Gradually, I began to relax and fell asleep.

When I awakened, my mind was no longer numb. I tried to recall books I had read before that would have concepts applying to my needs at that moment.

I remembered that Hannah Whitall Smith's book *The Christian's Secret of a Happy Life* had a chapter titled "Is God in Everything?" She believed that as Christians we must face the difficulty we all have of seeing God in everything. She wrote:

> People say, "I can easily submit to things that come from God; but I cannot submit to man, and most of my trials and crosses come through human instrumentality." . . .
>
> What is needed, then, is to see God in everything, and to receive everything directly from His hands, with no intervention of second causes. . . .
>
> Second causes must all be under the control of our Father, and not one of them can touch us except with His knowledge and by His permission. It may be the sin of man that originates the action, and therefore the thing itself cannot be said to be the will of God; but by the time it reaches us it has become God's will for us, and must be accepted as directly from His hands. No man or company of men, no power in earth or heaven, can touch that soul which is abiding in Christ, without first passing through His encircling presence, and receiving the seal of His permission. If God be for us, it matters not who may be against us; nothing can disturb or harm us, except He shall see that it is best for us, and shall stand aside to let it pass.[3]

I took my Bible and began to read, beginning in Genesis, just the passages of Scripture I had underlined. As I read, a clear picture of the providential care of God emerged. Time and again, God had affirmed His faithfulness.

"I am with you and will watch over you wherever you go, and I will bring you back to this land. I will not leave you until I have done what I have promised you" (Gen. 28:15).

"He will cover you with his feathers, and under his wings you will find refuge; his faithfulness will be your shield and rampart" (Ps. 91:4).

"As the mountains surround Jerusalem, so the Lord surrounds his people both now and forevermore" (Ps. 125:2).

"For he guards the course of the just and protects the way of his faithful ones" (Prov. 2:8).

"Indeed, the very hairs of your head are all numbered. Don't be afraid; you are worth more than many sparrows" (Luke 12:7).

"Even to your old age and gray hairs I am he, I am he who will sustain you. I have made you and I will carry you; I will sustain you and I will rescue you" (Isa. 46:4).

"He tends his flock like a shepherd: He gathers the lambs in his arms and carries them close to his heart" (Isa. 40:11).

"Who through faith are shielded by God's power until the coming of the salvation that is ready to be revealed in the last time" (1 Pet. 1:5).

"Can a woman forget her nursing child, that she should not have compassion on the son of her womb? Yes, they may forget, yet will I not forget you. Behold, I have indelibly imprinted (tattooed) a picture of you on the palm of each of My hands" (Isa. 49:15-16, Amp.).

As I read, I began to feel renewed hope. One of my favorite writers is E. Stanley Jones. I turned to his spiritual autobiography, *Song of Ascents*. He had a chapter dealing with bearing the troubles of life. I found the chapter titled "When Does Your Song Sing?" He said:

Jesus took the worst thing that could happen to Him, namely, the cross, and turned it into the best thing that could happen to humanity, namely, its redemption. He didn't bear the cross; he used it. The cross was sin, and he turned it into a revelation of love; the cross was man at his worst, and Jesus turned it into God at His redemptive best.

The answer, then, is: DON'T BEAR TROUBLE, USE IT. . . . Take whatever happens—justice and injustice, pleasure and pain, compliment and criticism—take it up into the purpose of your life and make something of it. Turn it into a testimony. Don't explain evil; exploit evil; make it serve you. Just as the lotus flower reaches down and takes up the mud and mire into the purposes of life and produces the lotus flower out of them, so you are to take whatever happens and make something out of it.[4]

Further on in the chapter I found the illustration that I had never forgotten:

I sat in a car which had a sliding seat in front. The husband called to his wife in the back seat, saying, "Dear, please kick me forward." "Good," I said to myself, "if life kicks me, and it is bound to kick me, then I shall determine the direction—I shall make it kick me forward!"[5]

How do I allow it to kick me forward? I found a passage in Hab. 3:17-19 that seemed to point the way.

Though the fig tree does not bud
    and there are no grapes on the vines,
though the olive crop fails
    and the fields produce no food,
though there are no sheep in the pen
    and no cattle in the stalls,
yet I will rejoice in the Lord,
I will be joyful in God my Savior.
The Sovereign Lord is my strength;

He makes my feet like the feet of a deer,
he enables me to go on the heights.

Here is a writer who chose *joy anyway!* It did not depend on his circumstances. It was a choice. And that choice affected three things: (1) his attitude, (2) his actions, (3) his accountability. When we will to be joyful, it will mean bringing our thought life into harmony with our will. This will nurture our attitude, and our actions will be a joyous expression affirming that choice! Our accountability is evidenced by the realization that we may not be responsible for many of the things that happen to us, but we are responsible for our responses to them!

There it was. It was my responsibility to choose, and by His grace I didn't want to miss the joy. So I chose joy!

When a year and a half later, the doctor came carrying (rather carelessly, I thought!) a great big bundle wrapped in green and placed the baby in my arms, I knew a different kind of joy! He said, "Carolyn, meet your halfback!" (You see, if I cannot have a lot of them, I have a big one! Kevin weighed 10½ pounds!) I will never forget opening that green blanket and seeing that boy for the very first time. He was neither red nor wrinkled! He was half-grown—and beautiful! In that moment, the prayer that I had prayed when I first knew I was carrying a child again, came true.

When I had realized I was pregnant again, I had sought God's help. I knew that I might love a child I had conceived in love and borne within my body for nine months, more than the two little girls God had given me to raise. I asked Him to stretch my capacity to love in such a way that there would be no difference between the love I felt for Sharon and Susan and the love I would feel for my baby. I knew I needed His supernatural touch.

When the doctor placed Kevin in my arms, a sense of overwhelming love for him washed over me! And for the first time I knew what Vernon's first wife, Doris, had given up when she had died. She had left her precious girls in God's care, knowing she would not be there to see them grow into womanhood. At that moment, God placed a love in my heart that has grown until I love Sharon and Susan just as much as if I had conceived them and borne them within my own body!

A few years ago, a new friend came to our home. As she was leaving, she glanced at our family pictures hanging in our hall and asked about our children. I told her the ages of our children and then she said, "How long have you and Vernon been married?" It was a few years less than our oldest child, so I needed to explain! As I was briefly telling her our story, Kevin walked into the hall. He heard her say, "Well, then, Sharon and Susan are Kevin's half sisters, aren't they?" It struck me that I had never thought about that before, but I agreed that that was so.

After she left, Kevin, who had overhead our conversation, asked me to come into the family room, as he wanted to talk to me. I will never forget what he said. He pointed his finger at me and said, "Mother, when Mrs.——— was here and you were telling her our story, you agreed with her when she said that Sharon and Susan were my half sisters." With a firm voice he said, "Mother, I don't ever want to hear you say that again. Sharon and Susan are not my half sisters. They are my whole sisters!"

When he said that, the tears began to roll down my face, for I knew God had answered the prayer I had prayed at the beginning of my pregnancy—abundantly and above anything I could ask or think! Sharon and Susan had cared for Kevin with such love. And he returned their love. They had spoiled him as he was growing up. Sometimes it had been difficult to discipline him when he needed it, because they were so protective of him! God not only had stretched my capacity for love but also had done it in each member of my family!

As Kevin has grown up, he has brought so much joy into our lives. He's 6 feet 2 inches tall now, but when I see him, that same sense of wonder-filled love washes over me. How thankful I am for our son! God *has* brought joy out of tears!

"Making the decision to have a child is momentous—it is to decide forever to have your heart go walking around outside your body!" (Elizabeth Stone in *Village Voice*)

*"You will go out in joy and
be led forth in peace;
the mountains and hills
will burst into song before you,
and all the trees of the field
will clap their hands."*

ISA. 55:12

▬ıιı 10

Buried Pain

To be a witness does not consist in
engaging in propaganda, nor even in
stirring people up, but in being a living mystery.
It means to live in such a way
that one's life would not make sense
if God did not exist.[1]   CARDINAL SUHARD

I cannot remember the setting, the time of day, or what
room I was in, and this is unusual. In the past, when
something of such grave significance happened, it would
be as if a picture of the moment was indelibly imprinted
on my mind. Yet, I can remember my reaction. The crucial
moment began as I was studying in preparation for teaching my Bible study. As a resource book, we were using Dr.
David Seamands' book *Putting Away Childish Things*. It
was a new book at that time. I was preparing to teach the
second chapter, which is titled "The Healing of Memories."

As I read the chapter, a heavy weight settled in my
chest, and a burning seemed to go through my mind. I had
a hard time taking a breath. My eyes felt like dust particles
were scratching the surface. I had to put the book down. I
cleared my lap of the notebook and Bible and rose to my

feet. I sought any diversion I could find to put off further reading at this time. I thought of things I needed to do: run a load of laundry; two or three phone calls that needed to be made; begin preparations for the evening meal—anything to take my mind off what I was reading. But even after doing all these various chores, I still could not go back to the book. I don't remember what I did the rest of the afternoon, but I know I did not read the book! However, I could not forget what I had read. It churned around and around in my mind.

The words that Dr. Seamands said that tortured my mind were:

> But the subconscious mind can also be a tormenter, for it contains tremendous power for producing evil and misery. This especially relates to painful childhood memories. In trying to push them out of our minds, we actually bury them deeper and deeper, until they no longer can find a way out. As a result, the intense emotions we experienced but did not express, at the time the hurt occurred, have no way of being expressed now. Buried alive within our hearts, they retain amazing persistence and explosive power.

> While we may think we are free of those apparently forgotten torments, this is not the case, for submerged memories cannot be stored away in peace in the same way that the mind files pleasant memories. Instead, we have to keep closing the door again and again, refusing to let these painful memories into our conscious minds. Since they can't enter through the door of our minds, they disguise themselves and try to smuggle into our personalities through another door.[2]

He explained how people can live with these unresolved memories for years. But there may come a time when some catalyst will trigger the pain of the memory to such point that those hidden memories they have tried to bury for so long are awakened and activated.

When the dormant inner child of the past is thus aroused, he can take over the person's attitudes, reactions, outlook, and behavior. The submerged emotions rise up and express themselves in feelings of deep depression, rage, uncontrollable lust, inferiority, fear, loneliness, and rejection.

These painful memories are not automatically evicted or transformed by an experience of conversion or even by the filling of the Holy Spirit. They are not necessarily changed by growth in grace. In fact, these memories are often great hindrances to spiritual growth. And until a person receives deliverance from them, he does not really mature. It is as if one part of his person is in a deep freeze, or in a time machine. His body matures and his mind develops but that one particular area is still frozen. He remains a little boy, she is still a little girl, locked into that childhood stage of life.[3]

The pain of revelation ripped through my body and spirit. I had, at various times through life, but with seemingly more frequency in the last two years, experienced with intensity most of those emotions: depression, uncontrollable lust, a sense of inferiority, fear, loneliness, and rejection. Even though I had accepted Jesus as my Savior at an early age and been filled with the Holy Spirit as I have already told you, when these feelings would emerge, I was devastated. But now the window of my memory was thrown open, and I remembered the scene I had buried in that memory all these years. Could it be that God in His mercy felt I was ready to face it and come to healing? When it came back, I remembered it in startling detail.

It was nighttime. The headboard of my bed was against one wall, and there was a walk space between the foot of my bed and the other wall. There was a small table in the left-hand corner of that walk space, and the light was burning low. It threw its own shadow up against the wall. My parents were gone, and a baby-sitter was staying with me. She was the daughter of friends of my parents. The interesting thing is, I clearly remembered her parents' name, but not hers. She must have been in her teens, probably late teens, but she was a grown-up to me. I wanted her attention, caring, and affection. As I put the pieces of memory together, I realized I must have been around five or six years of age.

In my memory, I was lying on my bed when she came into my room and lay down on the bed beside me. She talked for a while about nonthreatening things, for I do not remember the conversation. But then she said to me, "Let's pretend! Wouldn't it be fun!"

Now that would have been interesting to me, for I used my imagination all the time to "play house" or "play church." It was a game to me. I entertained myself often this way. But I began to be uncomfortable because she drew closer to me on the bed. She was on my right, and she took her left hand and began to run her hand up and down my right arm, over my hand and gently over my fingers very slowly. She was talking all the time she was doing this, but I began to lose the train of thought, because I was nervous about what was happening. Her manner had changed in a way I did not understand. But even though I was uncomfortable, I was fascinated with her because she was a teenager.

She said, "Let's pretend we are at a party, and some boys come up to us and want to sit by us." She continued to set the scene as though we were playing a game. I don't remember all of her exact words, but the last part of the scene was that we were lying down somewhere near those boys, and they began to touch us. All the time she was describing this, she was touching me more and more intimately. She must have sensed my unease and discomfort, for she said, "Don't worry; you see, this is all just pretending." Somehow this was supposed to make me feel all right.

But it wasn't all right, and little as I was, I knew it. I was too young to get caught up in her grown-up games. I didn't understand what she was talking about, nor what she was doing. Then she began to touch me even more intimately, and suddenly, feelings that I had never experienced before were stimulated by her touch. It felt good, and I wanted it to continue, and yet I didn't! Then she took my hand to her body and wanted me to do the same to her that she was doing to me. She took my hand and touched her body intimately. I was repulsed and even slightly nauseated. The feeling she had stimulated in me was shut off as I pushed her away.

I do not know what happened after that. But in my mind's eye I can see myself lying in the quiet darkness later, feeling guilt, fear, and confusion, questions hurling through my mind. I felt alone, dirty, and ashamed. Why did she come to *me?* Why did this happen? She told me no one would believe me if I told. And I believed her. I was a victim in despair. I could not deal with it, so I buried it; I told no one. But it was there, reeking its havoc deep in my subconsciousness down through the years.

What happened after the memory blazed its way into my consciousness? Emotional chaos. Feelings so intense I can only describe them inelegantly as gut-wrenching. I collapsed in the chair and sobbed and sobbed, wondering how on earth I was going to be able to teach my class the next day. I could not share this; it would be a while before I could even share it with my husband and immediate family. "O God," I screamed out in my inner being. "Please help me! Please help me pull myself together enough to finish the lesson for tomorrow. And then begin to show me how to work through this, Lord. Jesus, I need

Your healing hand. I am totally unable to function unless You intervene through Your Holy Spirit. O Jesus, I need You so much!"

I had no answers to the questions blazing their pathway through my consciousness, but I did have a Heavenly Father who was my Creator and understood me in the deepest levels of my personality. I belonged to Him. Now I needed His help to learn how to bring these haunting memories to Him and allow Him to heal my pain.

In the days ahead as I tried to open my mind and heart to God, I was full of conflicting emotions and questions. I knew God was listening to my heart's cry, the One who through the years of crisis has proven himself as my Comforter, Guide, and Friend. The journey of healing has been painful and at times arduously slow. But God has gently led, teaching me to honestly discover the truth about myself and about Him in His loving way. Up until this time my energies, subconsciously, had been geared to avoid the pain of it all. Now, I had to walk right up to the reality and pain and learn the truth and embrace it so that I might be healed.

At that time people were just beginning to talk more openly about child sexual abuse and to understand its shattering effect upon children for the rest of their lives. I began to study. I learned that child sexual abuse "covers a broad range of sexually oriented activities which involve the child. These range from sexual exposure and fondling all the way to anal or vaginal penetration."[4] It was disturbing to discover that the largest percentage of those who are sexually abused experience the abuse from someone they know and trust.

As I studied, I was horrified with what I learned. Most perpetrators of sexual abuse are male, and nearly 94 percent of them are related to the abused child. An even more staggering statistic to me was that the majority of reported aggressors are regular church attenders. As Dr. Richard

Butman, clinical psychologist and associate professor of psychology at Wheaton College, writes: "It is difficult to measure someone's 'Christianity,' but researchers do report that adult males tend to be very devout, moralistic, and conservative in their religious beliefs."[5]

I found it is not unusual for survivors of abuse to have repressed these hurting memories so completely that there are large memory gaps in their personal histories. One radio interviewer commented that every time he had a guest on his program who was an expert on child abuse, he would ask them the same question. "What percentage of victims of sexual, physical, or emotional abuse do you feel have significantly or completely blocked the memory of it?"

He said invariably the consistent answer has been, "More than 70 percent!"[6]

This gave me some comfort in helping me understand why I had not told anyone and that I was not alone in this happening.

There is overwhelming evidence that child sexual abuse is almost always related to deep and lasting pain that may affect every aspect of life: physical, social, emotional, and spiritual. The intensity of the consequences of the abuse is often the result of four factors: (1) The correlation between the age difference between the child and the aggressor, and the amount of the coercion involved. (2) Sexual involvement with a family member is more disturbing than sexual experience with an unknown adult. (3) The younger the child when the abuse occurs, the more severe the psychological disturbance may be for them as an adult. (4) The response of caregivers to a child's revelation of incest or abuse affects the long-term impact of the experience.[7]

I found almost nothing written about the type of abuse I experienced. Because of this, I felt special pain. I felt anger at the person who had abused me because I felt so violated; and I was angry that because of her actions, I had had to deal with fears about my own sexuality. In all my reading, most of the information was given for male-female sexual abuse. Almost nothing was written about female sexual abuse. I knew this was because predominantly the abuse is done by males, but this did not help me. I suffered with fear and confusion as to why a woman would abuse me. Was there something wrong with me? Oh, the pain of this! As I was dealing with this, another incident surfaced in my memory.

I remembered that after Dave died, and I returned to school, a young woman on campus wrote me a letter that, while not exactly making a proposition, implied it. When I read it, I was physically nauseated. I didn't understand then why it affected me so deeply. There was set up in me a feeling of deep anxiety. I thought about my married life and knew that I had been happy in my sexuality and my sexual relationships with both Dave and now Vernon. I had not been troubled by homosexual urgings. Yet here, another woman had made an approach to me. Had she thought that because I was without sex now, I would be interested in an alternative? I was absolutely devastated! My heart cried out, "Why?" Why had this happened to me? But this time when it had happened, I was an adult, and I knew what to do.

I took the letter to the school dean of women and let her read it. I needed to have her reaction. Was I assuming something that was not there, or did she agree as to the intent of the letter? She agreed. I asked her to contact the girl for me and to make sure that she left me completely alone. I had heard that she might be a homosexual before this, and I did not want to contact her myself in any way. I was never contacted again about the whole issue. One day I realized the girl was no longer at school, but I do not know when she left.

I knew the next step in my healing had to deal with

my anger toward my abuser. I have never seen the girl from that day on. I have no idea where she is. When I later shared my abuse with my father, he had no idea where she was either.

It was traumatic to share this experience with my father. Since my mother had Alzheimer's, I could not share it with her, and I knew my experience would be difficult for Dad to hear for several reasons.

1. He would feel responsible because my abuser was the daughter of a friend, and he had hired her.
2. Though as a minister, he had counseled others for years about many situations, it is different when it is your own family. It's hard to believe this could happen to you when you have tried to do your best as a parent.
3. His generation did not talk about this kind of thing, and it would be difficult for him to understand why I would feel I should share it with others.
4. I felt he would not understand how this could have been suppressed in my subconsciousness for so many years.

In fairness, I must say that abuse is difficult to deal with for *everyone* in a family. I knew this, but I needed their love, understanding, and support.

My father responded in all the above ways, expressing almost total denial. He even felt at that time it might be a figment of my imagination. This threw me into emotional despair so acute I knew I could never *write* about it.

One night, I could not sleep. Slipping quietly out of bed, I went into the living room to my favorite green chair. I questioned myself as to my own sanity concerning this. Did it really happen? But then I knew. Pain—wrenching, tearing pain—swept from the top of my head to the bottom of my feet as I recalled the scene again. No one would want to make up such an incident as this and subject themselves to such pain. I recalled, too, all the symptoms that verified its impact on my life. I knew it was real, and the conviction grew stronger that I must share it. Maybe it would help someone else come to healing.

Later, as Dad came to understand, he has been totally supportive in my writing. Vernon and my children and other family members have given freely of their love to support and understand. This helped me in my process of healing immeasurably.

I came to the point when I could sincerely pray and ask the Lord to help me forgive my abuser. I knew that if I could forgive her, I would be released from the power of this memory to devastate and control me.

But it seemed I was unable on my own to pray through to victory, and I realized I needed help. A friend of mine who is a Christian psychiatrist was willing to listen to my story. She recommended that the two of us, together in prayer, go back to that moment in my memory and allow God to show me myself as that young, innocent child—to feel again the emotions she experienced; to visualize her in that terrible moment, gazing up at the love-filled face of Jesus looking at her; to see His understanding that that moment was the result of the sin of another, and she need bear no guilt or shame. With the psychiatrist's counsel and prayer, I made it through those excruciating memories, vividly aware of the loving presence of Jesus sharing my pain as an innocent little girl, and bringing me to a point where in His presence I could forgive. This could only be brought about by His divine action in my life. And forgiveness brought release from the anger and prison of unforgiveness.

One of the difficulties that a victim of abuse will suffer is her own self-judgment at being a coparticipant in the sexual encounter. It must be stressed that a child victim is *free* of any responsibility. The aggressor is fully responsible! This is the pivotal point necessary to healing for the abused.

I know that I suffered also because my sexual arousal system had been prematurely activated. I was forced to deal with emotions and physiological responses that God did not intend for me to experience until later in my teen years.

Though I never told my parents of the abuse at that time, I did reach out to my mother for emotional support as a child. My mother was unable to be too active many times because of blood problems with her legs, and she had to rest in bed. I owe much of my mental health to her. It is because of her openness to me that I was able to have healthy friendships with women through the years, untouched by terrible scars in that area of my life. Many hours were spent by her bedside as I poured out my thoughts to her; and she counseled me, led me to Scripture, prayed for me, and loved me.

One of the most devastating effects of the abuse upon me was dealt with in Dr. Seamands' book, and I believe it was this statement that wrenched open my heart and mind to the memory of the abuse.

> Some people, who in their present lives are very sincere Christians, experience a near hypnotic, propulsive, and compulsive lust in their lives. Their imaginations paint terrible pictures on the walls of their minds, driving them into guilt and depression, and almost to self-destructive actions.[8]

When I read this, I felt I would come apart. For me, this humiliating experience had not manifested itself with this intensity until two or three years before my memory of the abuse surfaced. It was as though the memory was struggling to get through to consciousness with greater energy, and it attacked me in this way. There would be long periods of rest, and then suddenly I would be assailed by the kind of lust he described; then it would be followed by guilt, depression, and a feeling that God had forsaken me. I would be so whipped by it all, and desiring to be only pure in my thoughts and life, that there were times when I did nearly give up in despair.

Satan tried to defeat me during these times by attacking my self-image. I literally bathed my mind and spirit in Scripture to defeat him. I studied about God, both in Scripture and religious books dealing with developing a concept of God. I discovered *anew* that as anxious as I was to know Him, He was even more anxious to reveal himself to me. I saw that through the process of dealing with life's crises that I had experienced, He had used them to build my faith and to help me come to a healthier concept of myself. What Satan has tried to use to destroy me, God has used to open my heart to an understanding of myself. This has brought healing and wholeness.

I have experienced an excessive need for affection and the assurance of love. This is often a characteristic of abuse victims. This has been a difficult demand on my marital relationship. While Vernon is strongly supportive and shows his love in many ways, he has felt inadequate at times to be as verbal or affectionate in his expression of his love as I have sometimes needed him to be. We have worked at keeping the lines of communication open between us in order to make our way through this area of our relationship. I believe our love for each other has deepened as we have tried to understand the needs we both have in this area.

I have had a deep commitment to allow God to bring me to healing, *no matter how hurtful the journey*. Psychotherapist Susan Forward says:

> Revealing a major trauma . . . is just the beginning . . . People sometimes find so much relief in the initial revelation that they leave treatment prematurely . . . When the initial euphoria wears off, the patient is still struggling with unresolved conflicts . . . Emotional purgings need to be experienced repeatedly.[9]

We must go beyond the feelings of relief and follow the steps to wholeness.

I am following the steps to healing through personal responsibility. Some parts of my healing have happened instantaneously, but most have taken time. I have had to work through things in the loving presence of the Lord, consciously allowing Him to gently reveal truth about myself as He feels I am able to bear it. But He is there. The things I have learned have been life-changing. I have been fortunate that my experience happened only one time. I do not bear the scars of multiple instances of abuse. I did not have to live in close proximity to my abuser. It was not a close family member. All of these factors have been significant in my healing.

In coming to the point of the acceptance of the reality of the abuse, I have been able to say, "Yes, it did happen, but it's not my whole story." It's only a part! Jesus has given me hope that He is redemptively working!

If you have been a victim of child sexual abuse, or if you are wondering if the symptoms you are experiencing are indicative of abuse, please go to someone for help—a pastor you trust, a professional Christian counselor, or a trusted friend or family member. There are some excellent books available to help you to understand child sexual abuse. I have listed some at the back of this book.

Be honest. Face your problem. Determine to deal with it responsibly. Seek an abuse survivor's group. Begin personal Bible study and prayer. When you are able, begin using this experience redemptively by helping some other abuse survivor.

This has been a most difficult chapter to write. I feel as though my spirit is raw. There were times before I began to write, and even as I was writing, when I would think, I cannot, I will not, write it! The pain would be so acute. But I knew I would not be honest with my basic thesis if I did not share it. I would be saying, "Sorry, there is one reality you cannot face and know that God will be there to help."

There has come an inner joy once again as I, with awe and wonder, ponder God's transforming power in my life—though at times as I have been writing this chapter, it has seemed as if events around me were conspiring to prevent me from finishing my task. I have had a special awareness of His interceding power as I have tried to do what I felt He would have me do.

May that very same power bring healing and joy to you!

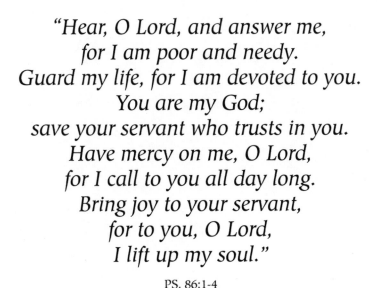

"Hear, O Lord, and answer me,
for I am poor and needy.
Guard my life, for I am devoted to you.
You are my God;
save your servant who trusts in you.
Have mercy on me, O Lord,
for I call to you all day long.
Bring joy to your servant,
for to you, O Lord,
I lift up my soul."

PS. 86:1-4

Uncharted Passage

There is no pit so deep that God's love
does not go deeper still.   **BETSY TEN BOOM**

It was time for dinner, and I called my mother and father, who were visiting, to the table. Mother walked into the kitchen slowly, and I directed her to her chair. It was difficult for her to negotiate this simple procedure. She didn't seem to know how to do it. She was 5 feet 10 inches tall, so her legs were long, and she could not remember how to swing them around and under the table. Dad had to help her. When it was all accomplished, she heaved a sigh of relief and gave me the most beautiful smile! As I was standing by her chair, I leaned over and gave her a hug.

But I was inwardly shattered, shocked into the awareness of how serious Mother's condition was. My father had explained to me about Mother's memory loss and deterioration of coordination and manual skills; but it is one thing to hear about them over the phone, and quite another to see them before your eyes. My parents lived in Texas, and lately Mother had not wanted to come up to see us because she was embarrassed about what was happening to her.

My mother was an elegant lady. By nature she was

quiet and shy, but she had a captivating sense of humor. She loved to tease. Always so gently feminine, she was a wonderful role model for my sisters, Jeanne and Kathleen, and me. She had soft blue eyes, and when she smiled, she was beautiful.

But I could see the difference. She didn't remember how to use the fork and knife. She took her glass and sat it in the middle of her plate in the middle of the food. When you would quietly remove the glass to its proper place on the table, or switch the utensils for her, she would look up as if to say, "Oh, yes! That's the way it's supposed to be!" and give you that wonderful smile again. She was very quiet during the meal and did not contribute much to the conversation, though she would respond occasionally with laughter at the appropriate time.

That evening after my father had helped her to get to bed, he came and talked with us. He said that Mom's mental deterioration seemed to be progressing more rapidly now than it had during the last year and a half. He asked if we had noticed how she did not talk very much at dinner. When we said yes, we had noticed, he said she didn't talk much anymore because she was aware of her memory loss and didn't want to repeat stories over and over again. He said he did all the cooking at home now because she could not remember the process anymore. He said he first noticed her difficulty one day when she baked bread. Mother had been known for her delicious home-made bread. She had made it for so many years, she no longer used a recipe. She loved to make bread. But one day, she forgot some of the ingredients and did not realize it. And when she was kneading the bread, she seemed to forget how to do it. With great struggle she finally got it into the pans to raise. But when she baked it, it did not raise very high, and it was hard. She knew she had left out some necessary ingredients. That was the last bread she baked. And this was difficult for her to deal with because it was a part of a loss of self.

My father shared with us that night his fear that Mother may have Alzheimer's disease. We were devastated just at the possibility!

Later, I would discover in my research about Alzheimer's the book *The Loss of Self,* by Donna Cohen, Ph.D., and Carl Eisdorfer, Ph.D., M.D. They say:

> In recent years the brain disorders of later life have become a personal tragedy in millions of lives throughout the world. Both the victim and the family suffer with the inexorable dissolution of self. Loss of sight, hearing, an arm, or a leg challenges a person to cope with significant change. However, the victim of Alzheimer's disease must eventually come to terms with a far more frightening prospect—the complete loss of self. And for the family, according to one daughter, "the death of the mind is the worst death imaginable." Family members share a life of emotional turmoil as they witness the disintegration of someone they love.[1]

We would find this to be true! We didn't know very much about the disease, but what we did know brought pain. As I researched, I also discovered:

1. There is no known cure as of this writing.
2. Diagnosis takes time; and no known medical tests available at this time can diagnose Alzheimer's disease with complete certainty during the life of the individual.
3. It is difficult for victims to recognize that they have a problem. The denial is strong. Family denial can also delay diagnosis.
4. The rate of progression of the disease is variable. Patients can go from health to the terminal stages in a couple of years; others survive longer than a quarter century.

5. True remissions do not occur in Alzheimer's, though there may be fluctuations in the pace of the disease.
6. Genetic vulnerability is not known.
7. Alzheimer's is irreversible.

My father had decided to move from Texas to Kansas City, as my sister Jeanne and I live here. Since communication with Mother was becoming more and more difficult, he was lonely. We wanted them to move so that we could help him with her care. They had come to look at several houses, and Mother seemed to be excited about seeing them. She had wanted to move up here for quite a while. We were glad that she seemed to have some limited understanding of what was happening.

One afternoon Vernon and my dad went to look once again at the house Dad had decided to buy. I felt as if I was coming down with the flu, and so I had taken some medication that made me sleepy. I had to keep Mother in sight, because she could wander off or harm herself in some way; so I had her sit in a chair near the couch where I was resting. But she was restless. She would pick up one of the magazines I had put near her, turn a few pages briefly looking at the pictures, and put it down. I knew she was feeling frustration, now that she could not completely comprehend what she was reading. She liked to look at the pictures, but they didn't convey meaning to her.

I must have dozed off a little because suddenly I became aware that she was walking around my couch. I jumped up and said, "Mother, where are you going?"

She turned to look at me with a puzzled expression, as if she couldn't quite figure out who I was. And then she said: "I'm looking for my husband. Where did he go?"

I said: "Mother, he went with Vernon to look at that house again. He'll be home soon." Just then, we could hear the garage door going up. Mother went to stand at the kitchen doorway, looking toward the back hall. When the door opened, and my father walked into the kitchen, she stared at him intently for a moment. Then she walked over to him quickly, threw her arms around him, and kissed him passionately! When she finished, my dad said: "My, what did I do to deserve that!"

My mother impishly laughed and said: "I call them like I see them. When I recognize him, I kiss him!" While Dad blushed, we all laughed delightedly. She had not lost her sense of humor!

The next day when we were alone, Mother tried to talk to me about what was happening to her. My father had prepared me. He told me that Mother was no longer able to play the piano or violin in public. She had had a humiliating experience recently. The pianist in her home church was not there, so she had been asked to play the piano for the congregational singing. She had been playing the piano all her life. But as she played that morning, she could not remember how to transfer the music she read to her fingers. She could not even remember how to play by ear as she had always done. She had to stop in the middle of the song. One person had made a disparaging remark about it, and my mother had been embarrassed and hurt. As a result, she had been afraid to play her violin publicly also. Her violin had been a source of pleasure and comfort to her for years. She was an accomplished musician. But now, even that seemed to be slipping away from her. The further loss of self was excruciating to her.

With halting phrases she tried to tell me about what had happened, and because I already knew, I could help her. I reached across to her and took her hand, trying to comfort her as the tears slipped down her face. She said, "My friend Naomi Larsen told me to keep on practicing to hold on to my music. I am going to go upstairs to my room now and practice. I'm determined to play as long as I can!"

Slowly, and laboriously, I helped her climb the stairs to her room. As I was preparing the evening meal, I could hear her tune up her violin. Then she began to play. She would play a song for a little bit, and then she would forget the rest. But she did not give up; she kept going over and over it, until she would remember a little more. Before, her music had been smooth and melodic; now her lack of dexterity made the bow screech, and the notes were not quite true. She kept playing for about half an hour. It was more than I could handle. My mother's violin playing was one of the sweetest memories I've had of my childhood. Tears rolled down my face as I listened to her. What a gutsy lady! I thought. Most people would have given up, but she is determined to be a part of life as long as she can!

On the return trip to Texas, when they stopped at a motel, suddenly Mother did not know who Dad was again. This can be difficult to deal with when you have been married for more than 50 years! Because she did not know him, she would not let him sleep with her! She put her clothes on over her nightgown and tried to leave the room. My father had to put a chair in front of the door and sit in it to prevent her from leaving the room. Finally, around 12:30 A.M. he called me.

He asked if I would speak to her. "Mother," I said quietly, "this is Carolyn. Are you sitting down?"

"No!" she said in a very agitated tone. "I cannot stay in this room with this man. I need to leave right now."

"Are you standing beside a bed?" I asked her.

"No," she said nervously. "I cannot stay alone in this room with this man. I need to leave right now!"

"Are you standing by a bed?" I asked her.

"Yes," she said.

"Would you sit down on it so that I may talk to you for a moment?"

It was silent for a few moments, and then I asked, "Are you sitting down now?"

Her still agitated voice said, "Yes, I'm sitting down."

Then for the next few moments I tried to gently suggest she take off her coat and lie down. It would be all right to sleep with her dress on over her nightgown if that would make her feel better. She needed the rest. She asked me what that man would do. I suggested that she could let him lie there. I told her that though she did not remember who he was, she did know him. I told her she would probably remember tomorrow that he was her husband. She seemed to gradually calm down.

My father was so tired. I tried to cheer him up by saying to him, "Daddy, she may forget who you are, but she hasn't forgotten her morals!" Thankfully, she did go to sleep, and the next morning she seemed to be willing to go along with Dad, even though she still didn't know him; he was security to her.

Watching the mental deterioration of someone you love is devastating. As one author put it: "No matter how saintly a person wants to be, and no matter how much one loves the victim of Alzheimer's disease, human beings are made of flesh and blood and not of spring steel. . . . It is absolutely essential that as much as possible, family members need to support the primary caregiver."[2]

We were anxious for my parents to move. Mother was physically and psychologically wearing on Dad. He needed our support. The irreversibility of the disease was devastating. Because there were times when she would seem to be better, you would take hope! But you would soon be shockingly aware again that she would never be better. The emotional roller coaster was heartrending.

One of the inescapable realities of the situation is that you have no idea how long the duration of the illness may be! Besides watching your loved one lose her sense of self, you worry about your financial ability to withstand this crisis. Also, it may be difficult for the primary caregiver to accept the reality that he will not be able to go without help. Over the years, my father had taken care of my mother faithfully through her health difficulties. We knew it would be very difficult for him to surrender her to someone else's care.

At Christmastime, my parents returned to Kansas City to spend the holiday with the family. My father had made arrangements with doctors here to put my mother through the necessary diagnostic tests to verify her illness. They validated that as far as they were able to determine, Mother did have Alzheimer's disease. She did comprehend the diagnosis. Because she felt there was a stigma attached to it, she was embarrassed for everyone to know.

One evening after the evening meal, Jeanne, Mother, and I were sitting in the kitchen talking, when suddenly we noticed that tears were slipping down Mother's face. Our hearts clutched with pain as we reached to hug her. Jeanne asked, "Mother, what is the matter?"

She was crying over the finality of the verdict. But we tried to give her hope by telling her of the variability of the disease and that some people keep their mental faculties to a certain extent for a fairly long time. We told her we would always be there for her, and she would never go through it alone.

Later on in the evening, she was sitting quietly in the living room in our pastel flame-patterned chair in the corner. We looked over at her and noticed she was sitting there with an intense look on her face. We asked her if there was anything wrong. She said, "No, I'm just sitting here trying to take a picture of all my family in my mind so that I will not lose it."

The first weekend of March, Vernon and I spoke at a retreat near Washington, D.C. I received a call telling me Mother was in intensive care near her home in Texas, and it looked to be a life-threatening situation, possibly a stroke. Instead of flying home, I boarded the plane for Dallas. My sister Jeanne and Chuck, her husband, arrived at nearly the same time from Kansas City. My sister Kathleen, who was already in Texas, met our plane and drove us to the hospital a couple of hours away.

In very serious condition, Mother was having a tremendous struggle breathing through a tube in her throat when we arrived. For the next two days it was a very traumatic situation. I believe Mother comprehended that we were all there. I rented a room in the hospital so that we'd all have a place to rest if we needed to, and I spent the nights there.

The moving van had been due to come that week to move my parents to Kansas City. My dad decided to send his furniture as planned. On the third day, in consultation with the Texas doctor and our doctor in Kansas City, it was decided that since Mother's breathing was better, she could be moved by private plane to Kansas City from the small hospital. Mother took the trip surprisingly well. We took her immediately to a hospital for a day or so before moving her to a nursing home.

The next few months were heartbreaking. Dad went to see Mother three times a day. He fed her lunch and dinner. We all tried to be with her as much as we could. She seemed to respond wonderfully well to her new surroundings, and the crisis seemed to be past. But she required total care now.

One difficulty with this disease is that you never know how you will find your loved one. She may know you and be very responsive, or she may not know you at all. Victims seem to have no short-term memory. Mother would tell me that Dad had not been there to see her—when he had just left. But she could still remember some things from the past.

Communication is difficult. We learned the following tips for communicating with Mother:

167

1. Touch gently and establish eye contact; do not startle.
2. Use gestures to reinforce verbal communication; hold hands out, smile, hug.
3. Be attentive to any message communicated by the patient's body position and movement.
4. Find a quiet setting; reduce environmental confusion.
5. Speak in concise, clear sentences.
6. Take advantage of calm moments to express warmth and caring with a gentle touch.
7. Aberrant behavior is less likely to be motivated by unconscious conflicts than by needs or fears.
8. Listen to the patient, even though her words do not make sense.
9. Construct sentences using words the patient uses.
10. Keep the voice calm, low, and reasonably modulated.
11. If unable to attract the patient's attention, leave and try again in a couple of minutes.
12. The patient may respond to verbalization very slowly; allow sufficient time.
13. Avoid talking as though the patient is not there. It is so easy to do without realizing it. Be sensitive to her personal dignity.[3]

The first time Mother looked at me without any recognition and a hostile expression when I called her Mother, I left the room crying. It seemed to distress her for me to call her Mother if she did not know me. She would look at me with such an intense expression on her face, trying to decide who I was. The awareness that she could respond hostilely to me was so out of character to the mother I knew, I could not comprehend it! One day, she had been sitting in her wheelchair with her head almost down on her chest, not responding at all, when suddenly she looked up at me and said, "I thought I was going to die, and I didn't want to at all!"

I said, "You mean when you were in Texas, Mother?" and she nodded her head. Then with tears slipping down her cheeks, she said, "Why is God allowing this to happen to me?" With my own tears running down my face, I answered, "I don't know, Mom, but when we get to heaven, we will be able to ask Him about it." For the moment she was satisfied.

Later, Mother went into a depression that tore at our hearts. It was so uncharacteristic of her. But one blessing we had is that her personality never became aggressive or violent, as Alzheimer's sufferers sometimes can. She remained her sweet, gentle self, and the nurses loved her wistful smile.

Two weeks before she died, I had a wonderful few moments with Mother that I felt was a love gift from God. We could see that she was deteriorating rapidly. She was in no pain, but her moments of cognizance were few. She had lost so much weight, and her body seemed to be shutting down.

I was sitting beside her bed, just holding her hand and gently rubbing her arm, when she turned her head and gave me a beautiful smile and with her blue eyes shining said, "Oh-h-h-h!" in recognition of me, and that was all. I stood up beside the bed, and taking her sweet face between my hands, I told her how much I loved her, and that she was the best mother that a girl could have had. I told her that I had realized while she was ill that she had been the most significant person in my life while I was growing up. All my other relationships in life were enriched because of her tender involvement in shaping my perceptions of life. She had given her love so freely to me, and I would never be able to thank her enough for the life she had lived before me. From her I learned how to be a Christian wife and mother. When I finished speaking, she looked me directly in the eye and smiled so sweetly with understanding, that I put my face down to her cheek, and our tears mingled together. That was the last time she knew me.

Though you can attempt to prepare emotionally for a loved one's death, you are never ready. Mother died February 21, 1991, at the age of 81. In the months of grief following, so many friends have been a part of my healing.

God led me to the story of the paralytic whose friends brought him to the house where Jesus was healing all who needed His touch. There was such a crowd they could not get in the door. So they climbed to the roof and made a hole large enough to lower him through it. Each man took a corner of the blanket and lifted the man down through the hole in the roof into the presence of Jesus. "When Jesus saw their faith, he said to the paralytic, 'Son, your sins are forgiven'" (Mark 2:5).

During this time of grief many have picked up the corners of the blanket and lifted me into the presence of Jesus for His wonderful healing comfort and touch. I am rich because of their love!

"For you have been my hope,
O Sovereign Lord,
my confidence since my youth.
From birth I have relied on you;
you brought me forth
from my mother's womb.
I will ever praise you. . . .
Do not cast me away
when I am old; do not forsake me
when my strength is gone."

PS. 71:5-6, 9

What Is That to Thee?

And nothing but our trials and perils would
ever have led us to know Him as we do,
to trust Him as we have, and to draw from Him
the measures of grace which our very extremities
made indispensable.[1]   A. B. SIMPSON

Dr. Richard Parrott never just walked to the pulpit when
it came time to preach; he would spring up from his chair
and stride to the center of the platform. You knew that he
had been waiting for just this moment. He had a word
from the Lord, and he could hardly wait to share it. This
particular day his text was taken from John 15:4-16. He
quoted the scripture, and then he made this statement:
"There is an incredible difference between living *in* Christ
and living *for* Christ!"

I didn't hear another word! That sentence burned its
way into my mind. What *was* the difference? Had I been
living *in* Christ or had I been living *for* Christ? I felt God
was trying to tell me something. Have you ever noticed
how when He is leading you into new truth, He will use
two or three witnesses to get your attention? Perhaps you
will be reading a Scripture passage, and He will speak to
you through a particular verse. Then you can be in a con-

versation with a friend who will talk about the same concept and give you some more food for thought. Then, you go to church on Sunday, and God has talked to your pastor too!

I found myself meditating on the question wherever I would be. I began to write down thoughts that came to me on whatever paper happened to be handy.

About this time, the headlines, news broadcasts, and talk shows were filled with a scandal that had struck the religious world. My first reaction was one of deep sadness. What a tragedy to see the testimony of a Christian tarnished or the cause of Christ damaged.

A real moment of discernment came for me when the parties involved were interviewed on the "Nightline" program. As I heard these people (who seemed to have started with a sincere desire to serve the Lord) defend themselves, I became so deeply distressed. How easily they had picked up the value system of our day. Even more frightening was the realization they were not cognizant of it and didn't recognize their jeopardy!

As I listened to the interview, the Holy Spirit began to help me identify several spiritual principles that had been violated. I felt that He was convicting my own heart on some of those same principles. It was my first step in the process of understanding the difference between living *in* Christ and living *for* Christ.

These are some of the principles I began to see:

1. The requirements for spiritual leadership are different from the requirements for leadership in the secular world. For the Christian there must be a purity of heart and actions that reflect Jesus Christ. We will see no redemptive results in our lives without it. The standards of our secular culture are not high enough for the believer. We cannot have three lives: a public life, a homelife, and a secret life!

A few years ago, David Hartman interviewed Mother

174

Teresa on "Good Morning America." He said to her, "Mother Teresa, you go out into the gutters of the streets of Calcutta. You reach down and pick up the dregs of humanity and take their dirty faces in your hands and give them love and a sense of personal dignity they have never had before. How do you do it?"

It was quiet for a few seconds before she answered. Her head was down in contemplation, the simple white habit with its wide blue band framing her face. But then she looked up, and her direct, piercing eyes looked into the camera as she said to David, "Mr. Hartman, you must have a pure heart, for only then can you see the face of God in another human being!"

As we gradually assimilate the value system of the secular world, our priorities become unclear. We begin to rationalize. We overlook the safeguards we have cherished because we don't think we need them any longer. How can we prevent compromising our way into error? Developing a sensitivity to the Holy Spirit's power as He checks our spirits when we err, and then acting in obedience, is our best defense.

2. Whatever ministry God gives us belongs to Him. We do not own it. It is His ministry, and He will use it to draw men and women to Jesus Christ. Ministry is not the reason for our life in Christ. We have life in Christ because He desires us to belong to Him.

A few years ago a brother in her order came to Mother Teresa, complaining about a superior whose rules, he felt, were interfering with his ministry. "My vocation is to work for the lepers," he told her. "I want to spend myself for the lepers."

She stared at him for a moment, then smiled. "Brother," she said gently. "Your vocation is not to work for lepers, your vocation is to belong to Jesus!"

I was so under conviction! I was teaching a large women's Bible study and teaching a Sunday School class.

I was speaking at retreats and conferences, but somehow without realizing it, I had gotten caught up in my "ministries"! I was possessive of them. They consumed my thoughts and time. How had this happened? How had I gotten so busy living *for* Christ that I had neglected living *in* Christ?

In his book *Power and Poise,* E. Stanley Jones says: "We are not called to be, but to belong. If it is 'to be' then that centers on the self; if it is to 'belong' then that centers on Christ. The catalyst that moves us beyond the belonging to ourselves and into belonging to Jesus Christ is self-surrender."[2]

The gentle, persistent searchlight of God's love stripped away the spurious subterfuge and helped me see my need. This is such evidence of His love. He does not reveal to us our need to put us down, but to lift us up, to help us be better than we are.

3. Christians should establish an alarm system, red flags in their lives that act as a safeguard from harm. We can easily become wrapped up in just *doing* things *for* Christ instead of learning to live *in* Christ. When this happens, we run the danger of letting what we *do* be the value on which we base our personal relationship with Jesus. The secular world measures us by performance because the things we do are most visible. Similarly, we can unconsciously allow what we do to take first place in our lives. We view it as proof that we are active, vital Christians. To avoid this trap, should we stop doing things for Christ? No. But I believe Jesus is most concerned with the quality of our relationship with Him. What we do for Him is merely an expression of our life in Him.

What does the Bible say about living in Christ? John 15:4-7 says:

> Dwell in Me and I will dwell in you.—Live in Me and I will live in you. Just as no branch can bear fruit of itself without abiding in (vitally united

to) the vine, neither can you bear fruit unless you abide in Me.

I am the Vine, you are the branches. Whoever lives in Me and I in him bears much (abundant) fruit. However, apart from Me—cut off from vital union with Me—you can do nothing.

If a person does not dwell in me, he is thrown out as a [broken-off] branch and withers. Such branches are gathered up and thrown into the fire and they are burned.

If you live in Me—abide vitally united to Me—and My words remain in you and continue to live in your hearts, ask whatever you will and it shall be done for you (Amp.).

1 John 4:15-16:

Any one who confesses (acknowledges, owns) that Jesus is the Son of God, God abides (lives, makes His home) in him, and he (abides, lives, makes his home) in God. And we know . . . and believe . . . the love God cherishes for us. God is love, and he who dwells and continues in love dwells and continues in God, and God dwells and continues in him (Amp.).

These scriptures verify that I have to live in Him, connected to Him, or I lose His perspective on life. What a life-changing revelation!

As I meditated on these principles, the Lord showed me I had become possessive of *my* Bible study and *my* Sunday School class and *my* speaking ministry. I became aware of how devoted I was to the *cause* of Jesus, but how desperately I needed to focus on simply belonging to Him!

I confessed it all to the Lord. I asked His forgiveness and thanked Him for His convicting power. He helped me know what red flags I should put up in my own life to safeguard from this kind of harm again. I will not share those private insights because I believe that God knows each of our weaknesses and vulnerabilities and deals with each one of us uniquely. What may be necessary for me may not be for someone else.

Gordon MacDonald, in his book *Ordering Your Private World*, points out that John the Baptist had a clear sense of his mission in life. It is revealed in the scripture John 3:30: "He must increase, but I must decrease" (KJV).

No matter how many thousands of people came out to see John and to hear his message, he never forgot his place. He had been chosen to be the forerunner, nothing else. As Dr. MacDonald says: "He knew he was to be the best man, never the bridegroom!" Anwar Sadat, in his autobiography, *In Search of Identity*, declared that there were two great moments in a person's life: the day that they were born, and the day they knew why they were born! What a joy to know that I was born to *belong* to Jesus and to *know* Him.

What happens when we begin to walk this way?

1. The approval of others takes its proper place in our lives. As E. Stanley Jones urged, we learn to *glance* at others and to *gaze* at Jesus! We learn to do what we do, just for Jesus' sake and no other. Bob Benson once said, "At the end of a day what gives you the greatest sense of accomplishment—the feeling you've 'done good'—is it a result of what He did in you and His approval or what others did and what THEY said?" If it is the approval of others, we will always be disappointed!

In the flyleaf of my Bible I have written these words quoted by Hannah Whitall Smith: "Never indulge, at the close of an action, in any self-reflective acts of any kind, whether of self-congratulation or of self-despair. Forget the things that are behind, the moment they are past, leaving them with God."[3]

This means bringing to Him my insecurities as well as my pride and letting Him transform and heal me.

2. We learn to depend on the Holy Spirit's power to free us from a spirit of damaging comparison with others.

Gal. 6:4-6 says: "Each one should test his own actions. Then he can take pride in himself, without comparing himself to somebody else, for each one should carry his own load."

Peter, James, and John, the closest apostles to Jesus, were walking along with Him one day near the end of Christ's ministry. Jesus was telling Peter how he would die one day. In response, Peter pointed to John and asked Jesus how John would die. Jesus said to Peter, "What is that to thee?" (John 21:23, KJV). Have you ever wondered why God in sovereignty lifts some people up and honors them with fame and allows others to serve in obscure places where no one ever learns their name? The lonely missionary who serves unheralded in some tiny village in the jungle is just as pleasing to God as a world-renowned evangelist. The key is that we find God's will and do it! There is a deep, inner peace that comes when we believe we are fulfilling the purpose for which we were created! I hope that when I get to heaven and God shares the picture He had of what I could become in Him, it is not too far from what I actually became!

Paul says: "I have learned in whatever state I am, to be content" (Phil. 4:11, NKJV). It's a process to learn to leave the choice to God. When we live in Him, He transforms our minds and changes our personalities so that we develop attitudes that are not possible without His enabling power.

I'll never forget how this lesson was brought home to me.

It happened at a ladies' retreat in Chicago several years ago. I had been asked to conduct one of the seminars on the Saturday afternoon of the retreat. I would repeat the topic in two different sessions. This was the first time I have ever conducted a seminar. Prior to this I had always been the "featured speaker." As a result I was dealing with some new insecurities.

The featured speaker for this retreat was Nona Kelley, one of my closest friends, and I was honestly delighted to be on the same program with her. We drove from Detroit together and had five hours of nonstop, stimulating conversation along the way. I was expecting a fantastic time.

The retreat was held in a beautiful Chicago hotel. The Retreat Committee had planned everything with excellence, and there was a spirit of excitement everywhere. After checking into my room, I decided to locate the room where my seminar would be held. Outside the door was a nice sign with the seminar title and my name. On entering, I saw that it was a fairly large room. I hope someone comes to my seminar, or this room is going to seem awfully big! I thought.

The person who was coordinating the seminars walked into the room and said, "Carolyn, I would like you to prepare just a few sentences of introduction to your seminar for the meeting tonight. We will have all the seminar leaders come to the front and give a capsule view of their subject to whet the interest of the women."

My spirits plummeted! That would be so tough! But I hurried back to my room to work on my introduction. I wanted it to be good so that women would want to come. Suddenly, I found myself comparing my efforts with those of the other seminar leaders.

Before the evening session, there was a meeting for all the committee staff and speakers. As we gathered in the room, the other women looked so sharp and well-groomed. Suddenly, all my own inadequacies washed over me. Why did I say I would do this? I wondered. What if only a few came to my seminar? Would the committee look on me as a person who cannot draw a crowd and pass the word to other groups?

My mood had gone from joyful anticipation to near dread! I continued to size up the other women. They all seemed so confident. What were they thinking down inside? Was I the only one fighting feelings of inadequacy?

It is only natural at times for us to be thrust into situations where we feel inadequate. It happens to us all and is no reason to feel guilty. What concerned me was the overprotectiveness I felt for my reputation as a speaker. I was fighting an intense spirit of competition!

When they introduced the seminar leaders, we all marched to the front as they called our name. I was one of the first to give my brief introduction. When I finished, I stepped back into the line of women. After me, each person seemed to give a much snappier introduction, and I wanted to disappear. For the remainder of the evening I participated in all the activities, smiling and doing my best to be friendly and warm, but inside I desperately wanted to leave the crowd.

Finally, I was able to get back to my room. Dropping everything I was carrying onto the bed, I fell to my knees. I poured out my feelings to the Lord. I confessed to Him my despair that I was having such difficulty. I knew I was not responsible for the feelings coming into my heart, but I was responsible for how I respond to their presence. I asked the Lord to so cleanse me from any harmful pride that I could be genuinely happy for the good attendance others had in their seminars, no matter how many came to mine; I prayed it would not even be an issue of concern for me. I asked Him to anoint each seminar leader and speaker with His Holy Spirit as she spoke. I asked Him to give me a love for each person with whom I came in contact that weekend, love that would be deeper than anything I could have on my own. I asked Him to fill me so full of himself that His presence and His approval were all that I needed.

The next day, I went down to my room early. As I paused in the doorway, I asked the Lord to help each woman who entered there to feel His presence and to open her heart to Him. I walked between the aisles of seats and asked God to touch each woman so that when she left that room, the person she was most aware of was the Lord Jesus Christ. I gave Him my own inadequacy and thanked Him for what He was going to do. And then I relinquished it all to Him.

Peace and honest joy settled on my spirit. When it came time for the women to arrive, I walked to the door to greet them. I did not need to look down the hall to see how many were going to the other rooms—it did not matter!

I found it easy to speak because I had been freed from people and could focus on the message. When the seminars were over, I left the room humbled by the awareness that I could have missed it all. I could have been so wrapped up in the unimportant that God would have been limited in what He could do through me.

I learned another valuable lesson that day. When I am confronted with a need for God's help and power, I must not wait to pray. The answer to opening our lives to God's power is to go to Him *now*. When I first became aware of the wrenching emotions, I should have slipped off to a place to be alone and cry out to God for His help immediately! It need not be a long prayer. It's just opening our hearts to Him, talking to the One who has the power to transform any situation in miraculous ways.

Since then, I have tried to follow through on this. When in need, I have even slipped into the stall in the rest room where I could be alone to pray. God and I have laughed at some of the places I have found to be alone with Him—but it works! Praying *now* releases His power and teaches us to come to Him first before we go to anyone else.

I never did know how many people the others had in their seminars. When we got together, we were more interested in what we could learn from one another. But I do know that from that time on, I knew what to do when the "tyranny of competition" struck! When I sense those kinds of feelings trying to assail me, I seek God's help immediately, for I know He is able to give me victory.

3. We learn that there are times when the Lord will close the door on one ministry to open another, or close the door and leave you on the shelf for a while. If our "ministry" is totally surrendered to Him, He helps us in those moments to stay steady and wait.

Nobody has ever claimed that waiting is easy. But we learn that it is important to find not only His will but also His timing!

A few years ago, a friend of mine who is a speaker and writer shared with me this story. She has always loved to write and has had several books published. But for two years, God seemed to tell her that she should not write again until He released her. It was difficult for her because writing was a gift that He had given her, and she loved it. She wondered why He would give her a gift that He did not allow her to use. But later she realized that in those two years, she discovered that the purpose of her life was to learn to know Him. She said, "Carolyn, God has shown me how much I needed this time to go deeper into the things of God. Now I know that there were truths He wanted to teach me that He could not before, because I was too busy. I have released the writing to Him, and I have peace."

When she told me this, I thought, Oh, I hope God allows me to go on speaking. I've felt it was a God-given desire.

About a year ago, I looked at my datebook, and to my wonder I realized that about three months of the peak "retreat season" was not booked. I had always been booked at least a year in advance. Is God closing this door of ministry, I wondered? Is He beginning to release me?

I remembered my friend's words. I could either wait

and let God show me His will, or I could get uptight and possessive of ministry. As I was dealing with this in my own heart, it seemed I kept running into others who speak, and they shared their busy schedules with me. The Lord was expanding their opportunities, and it seemed He was closing mine.

I chose to surrender that time to the Lord to fill (or not to fill) as He chose, but to give me the grace to deal with His will. As the months unfolded, I was amazed to see how wise the Lord has been. He knew that during that time I would have an unplanned surgery that would have serious complications. I would not have been able to go anywhere speaking. Also, because of the surgery, my writing schedule for this book was set back, and I needed to make up for lost time. He knew how much I could bear!

At about this same time He had a blessing in store for me. One day as I was particularly stressed and trying to get things done, the phone rang, and a woman whom I did not know explained her reason for calling. She was from Memphis. She had heard me speak that spring at a conference. She said that as she was listening to me speak, the Lord said to her, "Thelma, I want you to take Carolyn Lunn as your special prayer interest in your prayer group." She was startled, for she did not know me. But she promised the Lord that she would obey His request. She didn't come and tell me about it because she was so unsure of what He was trying to do.

She went home and gathered her group together and explained what God had told her. They all decided to obey the Lord, and they began to pray for me. They often would put a chair in the middle of the group representing me and my needs and then gather around it and pray until God gave them peace. She had felt that now she could call me, because she felt God wanted them to pray even more specifically than they had been. She told me what a blessing had come their way because of their obedience and the wonderful presence of the Lord they had experienced. Did I have any special requests that I would want to share with them to enable them to pray more specially for my needs?

I could hardly believe my ears and was amazed at God's timing. I was overwhelmed by the love of my Lord, who would care so much for me that He would lift up a group of faithful prayer warriors from women I did not even know! It made me realize that He was actively involved in what was happening in my life. His precious will was being fulfilled. These precious ladies have been an uplift and source of power for God's working in my life. I can only be grateful that Thelma Westmoreland loved Jesus enough to obey Him and include me in their circle of love. It has been an affirmation to me for the path in which God has led me this last year. What joy I might have missed if I had not walked this unknown way, joy that only comes from walking in obedience with Him.

> To struggle used to be
> To grab with both hands
>   and shake
>   and twist
>   and turn
>   and push
>   and shove and not give in
> But wrest an answer from it all
> As Jacob did a blessing.
>
> But there is another way
> To struggle with an issue, a question—
> Simply to jump
>   off
>   into the abyss
>   and find ourselves
>   floating
>   falling

185

```
              tumbling
              being led
        slowly and gently
        but surely
        to the answers God has for us—
        to watch the answers unfold
        before our eyes and still
        to be a part of the unfolding.
But, oh, the trust
necessary for this way!
Not to be always reaching out
for the old handholds.
```

                    Susan Ruach
                    —"A New Way of Struggling"[4]

EPILOGUE

Tim Hansel, in his book *Eating Problems for Breakfast,* quotes Alfred Kazin, who says: "In a very real sense, the writer writes in order to teach himself."[1] This has certainly been true for me. Writing this book has been one of the most difficult challenges I have ever faced. If I had not deeply sensed that this was part of God's plan for my life, I could not have completed it.

The theme of the book has been: "You can walk right up to reality, no matter what it is, and know that God is there already before you, waiting to anoint you with the oil of His joy!" But it has seemed as though Satan has said, "Oh, so you really believe that, do you? Well, let's just see!"

I have had four major surgeries this last year and a half; my mother's illness accelerated its pace, and she died; and other testings came about which my pen will never be able to write. Some things that have always been securities in my life have been stripped away. But oh, the power and joy in the presence of my Lord in those difficult hours!

I have not been alone. The poem Carole Mayhall wrote in *Help, Lord, My Whole Life Hurts,* expresses this so clearly:

> *God is with me.*
> *God is in me.*
> *God is.*
> *God.*[2]

Jean Anglund said: "A bird doesn't sing because he has an answer; he sings because he has a song!"

I don't have all the answers, but I do have a song! And that song is: There is *joy . . . anyway!*

NOTES

Epigraph and Introduction

1. Lewis B. Smedes, *How Can It Be All Right When Everything Is All Wrong?* (New York: Harper and Row, 1982), 11, 15.

2. Tim Hansel, *You Gotta Keep Dancin'* (Elgin, Ill.: David C. Cook Publishing Co., 1985), 19.

Chapter 1

1. Hannah Whitall Smith, *The Christian's Secret of a Happy Life* (Old Tappan, N.J.: Fleming H. Revell Co., 1952), 63.

2. *Webster's Ninth New Collegiate Dictionary,* s.v. "joy."

Chapter 2

1. Ashleigh Brilliant, *Pot Shots* No. 1318 (Santa Barbara, Calif.: Brilliant Enterprises).

Chapter 3

1. Ron Lee Davis, *The Healing Choice* (Waco, Tex.: Word Books, 1986). Quoted in *Eating Problems for Breakfast* by Tim Hansel (Dallas: Word Books, 1988), 171.

Chapter 4

1. Catherine Marshall, *A Closer Walk* (Old Tappan, N.J.: Fleming H. Revell Co., 1985), 51.

Chapter 5

1. Oswald Chambers, *My Utmost for His Highest* (New York: Dodd, Mead and Co., 1935), 305.

Chapter 6

1. *Oswald Chambers—the Best from All His Books,* vol. 2, chosen and ed. Harry Verploegh (Nashville: Oliver Nelson, Thomas Nelson Publishers, 1989), 41.

Chapter 7

1. Tim Hansel, *Holy Sweat* (Waco, Tex.: Word Books, 1987), 33.

2. Hansel, *You Gotta Keep Dancin',* 73.

Chapter 8

1. Ibid., 80.

Chapter 9

1. Max Lucado, *No Wonder They Call Him the Savior* (Portland, Oreg.: Multnomah Press, 1986), 77.

2. Gail Sheehy, *Character, America's Search for Leadership* (New York: William Morrow and Co., 1988), 15.

3. Smith, *Christian's Secret of a Happy Life,* 148-49, 151-52.

4. E. Stanley Jones, *Song of Ascents* (Nashville and New York: Abingdon Press, 1968), 180, 183.

5. Ibid., 183.

Chapter 10

1. Madeleine L'Engle, *Walking on Water* (Toronto: Bantam Books, 1980), 31.

2. David Seamands, *Putting Away Childish Things* (Wheaton, Ill.: Victor Books, 1982), 18-19.

3. Ibid., 19-20.

4. Maxine Hancock and Karen Burton Mains, *Child Sexual Abuse* (Wheaton, Ill.: Shaw Publishing Co., 1987), 5.

5. Ibid., 12.

6. David Peters, radio interview with Rich Buhler, "Talk from the Heart," station KBRT, Nov. 19, 1986.

7. Hancock and Mains, *Child Sexual Abuse,* 32-33.

8. Seamands, *Putting Away Childish Things,* 22.

9. Susan Forward and Craig Buck, *Betrayal of Innocence: Incest and Its Devastation* (New York: Penguin Books, 1978), 166.

Chapter 11

1. Donna Cohen, Ph.D., and Carl Eisdorfer, Ph.D., M.D., *The Loss of Self* (New York and Scarborough, Ont.: New American Library, 1986), 22.

2. Gary D. Miner, Ph.D., and Linda A. Winters-Miner, Ph.D., *Caring for Alzheimer's Patients* (New York and London: Insight Books, Plenum Press, 1989), 95.

3. This is a composite list drawn from the above books and Nancy Mace and Peter Rabins, M.D., *The 36 Hour Day* (Baltimore and London: Johns Hopkins University Press, 1981).

Chapter 12

1. Mrs. Charles Cowman, *Streams in the Desert* (Los Angeles: Cowman Publications, 1955), 330.

2. E. Stanley Jones, *The Way to Power and Poise* (New York and Nashville: Abingdon-Cokesbury Press, 1949), 72.

3. Smith, *Christian's Secret of a Happy Life,* 202.

4. Rueben P. Job and Norman Shawchuck, *A Guide to Prayer for Ministers and Other Servants* (Nashville: Upper Room, 1983), 331-32.

Epilogue

1. Tim Hansel, *Eating Problems for Breakfast,* 7.

2. Carole Mayhall, *Help, Lord, My Whole Life Hurts* (Colorado Springs: Navpress, 1988), 88.

BIBLIOGRAPHY
ON SEXUAL ABUSE

Seamands, David. *Putting Away Childish Things.* Wheaton, Ill.: Victor Books, 1982.

Hancock, Maxine, and Karen Burton Mains. *Child Sexual Abuse.* Wheaton, Ill.: Shaw Publishing Company, 1987.

Littauer, Fred and Florence. *Freeing Your Mind from Memories That Bind.* San Bernardino, Calif.: Here's Life Publishers, 1988.

Frank, Jan. *A Door of Hope.* San Bernardino, Calif.: Here's Life Publishers, 1987.